Civil Liberties
A Beginner's Guide

ONEWORLD BEGINNER'S GUIDES combine an original, inventive, and engaging approach with expert analysis on subjects ranging from art and history to religion and politics, and everything in between. Innovative and affordable, books in the series are perfect for anyone curious about the way the world works and the big ideas of our time.

anarchism	forensic science
artificial intelligence	french revolution
the beat generation	history of science
biodiversity	humanism
bioterror & biowarfare	islamic philosophy
the brain	journalism
the buddha	lacan
censorship	life in the universe
christianity	machiavelli
civil liberties	mafia & organized crime
classical music	marx
cloning	medieval philosophy
cold war	middle east
crimes against humanity	NATO
criminal psychology	oil
critical thinking	the palestine–israeli conflict
daoism	philosophy of mind
democracy	philosophy of religion
dyslexia	philosophy of science
energy	postmodernism
engineering	psychology
evolution	quantum physics
evolutionary psychology	the qur'an
existentialism	racism
fair trade	the small arms trade
feminism	sufism

Civil Liberties
A Beginner's Guide

Tom Head

ONEWORLD

OXFORD

A Oneworld Book

Published by Oneworld Publications 2009

ISBN 978–1–85168–644–5

Typeset by Jayvee, Trivandrum, India
Cover design by www.fatfacedesign.com
Printed and bound in Great Britain by Bell & Bain, Glasgow

Oneworld Publications
185 Banbury Road
Oxford OX2 7AR
England
www.oneworld-publications.com

Learn more about Oneworld. Join our mailing list to
find out about our latest titles and special offers at:

www.oneworld-publications.com

*To my activism mentors
Shannan Reaze and Michelle Colón,
the two best guides any beginner could ask for.*

Contents

Acknowledgments

We're all shaped by other people, and at the most fundamental level this means my family. My mothers, Carol and Cappy, are more responsible than anyone else for making me who I am. My grandparents Maybelle and Robert Carwile, my father John, my brother Jim, my nephew Anthony – these are all people who also played a significant role in my intellectual development.

I would not be qualified to write, or interested in writing, a beginner's guide to civil liberties if it were not for the many excellent local activists I've worked with here in Mississippi. Chief among them are Shannan Reaze and Michelle Colón, to whom this book is dedicated; our adventures organizing direct action protests, leading issue advocacy in the media, and wrestling with the Mississippi State Legislature have been essential to shaping me as an activist. There are many, many other people who have guided me as an activist, but any attempt at a list would be dreadfully incomplete. Having no desire to hurt the feelings of any of my dear friends in the local activist community, I can only say that if you think I owe you my thanks, I almost certainly do.

My writing career has also been shaped by many people. Chief among them are the father–daughter writing team of John and Mariah Bear, who nine years ago brought me on board for a book project they were writing and transformed me from an aspiring author into a published author. If they had not made that generous decision, this book – and the other twenty-two books I've written, cowritten, or compiled over the years – would not exist.

Since March 2006, I've been running an online community and resource center on civil liberties for About.com, part of the New York Times Company. You can find it on the web at http://civilliberty.about.com, which is the place to go if you have something you'd like to ask me, or something you'd like to say, or if there's something you'd just like to find out more about. The people I've worked with at About.com – among them staff members Fred Meyer, Jennifer Hubley, Caryn Solly, Sue Funke, Susan Hahn, Daniel Levisohn, Lauren Leonardi, Eric Hanson, and the hundreds of fellow About.com guides who help make up our online community – have certainly shaped my development as a writer, and made it possible to produce this book.

This book is in your hands right now because of Marsha Filion at Oneworld Publications, who was an advocate for this project and helped shape it into what it is. Good editors are collaborators, coauthors in a sense, and Marsha is certainly a good editor. Her wisdom, patience, and attention to detail have been essential to this book.

Illustrations

1
Understanding civil liberties

> There will be no loyalty, except loyalty toward the Party.
> There will be no love, except the love of Big Brother ... All
> competing pleasures will be destroyed ... If you want a picture
> of the future, imagine a boot stamping on a human face –
> forever.
>
> (George Orwell, *Nineteen Eighty-Four*)

Liberty is power. I don't mean this in any metaphorical sense; I
mean, literally, that liberty is power, agency, room to spread
one's arms. Or as Thomas Jefferson put it: 'Rightful liberty is
unobstructed action according to our will within limits drawn
around us by the equal rights of others.' In a word, power.
Tyrants tend to have boundless liberty, which is what makes
them tyrants. Slaves tend to have very little liberty, which is
what makes them slaves. Assuming you live in a modern liberal
democracy or something approaching one, you and I don't have
or need as much liberty as tyrants, but we have more liberty than
slaves. I suppose that's something.

People don't talk much about the liberty of tyrants because
liberties, like your neighbor's pants, are most noticeable when
they're missing – and when you think about it, tyrants have a
great many liberties that most of us, even in liberal democratic
countries, will never have. A tyrant who wants something can
take it by force. A tyrant who wants to promote an ideology can
promote it using government funds, and imprison or kill

anybody who speaks out against it. If you're a tyrant, everything in the country you rule is essentially yours. You can have the best food, the best clothes, the best medical care. You never have to wait in line for anything. And if the best your country has to offer isn't good enough for you, you can always declare war on a neighboring country.

Figure 1 An Iraqi strikes a mural of former dictator Saddam Hussein with his shoe, which would have been a very dangerous thing to do before Hussein was deposed.

But it isn't really decent to want a tyrant's liberty, because that kind of liberty impedes the ordinary liberty of so many other people. So what kinds of liberty should we want? What kinds of liberty are we entitled to? And what kinds of liberty can we realistically protect? This book looks at, but does not definitively answer, these questions – because this book is a beginner's guide in both senses of the word.

Everybody is a beginner when it comes to civil liberties because everybody lives exactly one life, and one life can never contain the very different realities that individual people face when their civil liberties are violated. Odds are good that I'll never be sold into forced labor, or locked up for my religious beliefs, or beaten half to death by police officers for attending a protest. There are things I'll never understand viscerally, forms of oppression I'm not even aware of, and that means I'll always be a beginner. But I can listen, because that's what beginners do, and I can tell you what I've heard.

In Zen Buddhism, there is a value concept called *shoshin* – 'beginner's mind.' To have *shoshin* is to approach a subject with an open mind, with curiosity, with humility – to be a beginner, no matter how much one has studied the subject. Believing that we are no longer beginners – believing that we understand oppression in any comprehensive way – closes our ears to the experiences of strangers. It's fine to be an expert on civil liberties; I hope this book gets you started on that journey. But no matter how much of an expert you become, it's important always to remain a beginner, never to lose the capacity to listen.

The opposite of liberty

All laws have the same basic function: They restrict individual liberty by providing deterrents to undesirable behavior. This sounds like a bad thing at first, but some liberties are worth

Figure 2 Police raid the lunch room at 922 Pennsylvania Avenue in Washington, DC, looking for illegal liquor. Alcoholic beverages were illegal in the United States between 1920 and 1933.

restricting – the liberty to murder people at random, for example. There are also liberties that most of us agree should never be restricted – such as the liberty to air opinions publicly on policy issues, or the liberty to read whatever we want to read, or the liberty to worship (or not worship) according to our own belief systems. We refer to these basic liberties, the liberties to which we believe every person is entitled, as civil liberties. There is no easy step-by-step process, no simple ten-word definition, that can tell us which liberties constitute civil liberties. Personal definitions of civil liberties tend to vary depending on what sort of laws one believes should be passed.

Every law, every restriction on personal liberties, tends to be grounded in one or more of three basic principles. First, the harm principle: the most basic purpose of law is to protect people from each other. Laws against murder, rape, assault, robbery, burglary, fraud, and so forth are all generally based on the idea that the government has the authority to intercede against, and punish, those who intentionally inflict harm on others. Some form of the harm principle is honored in every legal system.

But even the harm principle can be used to justify excessively restrictive laws, given a sufficiently broad definition of harm. A law against hurting the feelings of others, for example, could be legitimately defended on the basis of the harm principle.

The harm principle protects people from both actual and potential harm. If someone drives under the influence of alcohol or narcotics, for example, then that person can be detained and/or punished under the harm principle simply because of the danger that this sort of behavior poses to the community.

But application of the harm principle in cases of potential harm can be incredibly restrictive. The indefinite detention of hundreds of Afghan prisoners by the US military at Guantanamo Bay, Cuba, for example, is defended on the basis that these prisoners – never convicted of any crime – *might* cause harm to others at a later date.

Second, the caretaker principle: most people also believe that governments have some obligation to protect them from harm even when that harm is not directly inflicted by others. In the ancient world of the Hebrew Bible, this protection was extended to orphans and widows – two classes of people who, by the standards of their time, had no visible means of support. Today, social policies guaranteeing access to food, shelter, education, and health care are justified on the basis of the caretaker principle.

The caretaker principle is also often used to restrict the availability of alcohol, tobacco, narcotics, and other things that citizens might use to hurt themselves. The danger of this is that anything that the government deems harmful can be subject to regulation – the life of a law-abiding citizen narrowed to an institutionalized and almost childlike state.

Third, the utopian principle: some policies are not about direct harm at all; they're about protecting the lawmakers' vision of how the society should function. Most laws restricting same-sex relationships, for example, are proposed on the basis of the lawmakers' utopian principle of a society in which everyone fits neatly into the institution of heterosexual marriage. Laws restricting displays of contempt directed towards flags or other national symbols are most often proposed based on the lawmakers' utopian principle that everyone *should* behave in a patriotic way, at least in public. Laws severely restricting immigration, or banning undesired languages, or discriminating against racial or ethnic groups, are generally also passed to fulfill the lawmakers' utopian goals.

The utopian principle is a fuzzy category, reflecting the fact that arguments based on the utopian principle are generally based on emotional appeal rather than abstract argument.

UTOPIAS AND DYSTOPIAS

Most people want to help create a better world, but few people are completely sure what that world would look like. Enter the utopian writers, who describe vastly superior worlds where our better social principles have triumphed:

- Sir Thomas More's *Utopia* (1516) defined both the word 'utopia' (meaning 'no place') and the concept of the utopian novel. Among the features of More's island of Utopia are a benevolent monarchy, socialism (all goods and resources are shared; there is no private property), large households (with ten to sixteen adults each), and slavery (each household has two chained slaves – usually criminals or prisoners of war).
- William Morris's *News from Nowhere* (1890) could best be characterized as describing a benevolent anarchy – there is no government authority and no police force, and everyone works for four hours per day on agrarian pursuits.
- B.F. Skinner's *Walden Two* (1948) describes a commune operating under the principles of his own system of behavioral psychology, in which each member of the society is inculturated into a happy, productive life.

UTOPIAS AND DYSTOPIAS (*cont.*)

- Gene Roddenberry's vision of a future world in the *Star Trek* television series and films (1966–present) is that of an Earth in which national rivalries no longer exist, war has been abolished, the human species has focused primarily on science, and the resulting technological advances have allowed humanity to expand throughout the universe, befriending kind aliens and defeating unkind aliens, progressing inevitably towards human perfection, enlightenment, and cosmic peace.

But for every viable utopia that can be imagined, there is also a viable *dystopia* ('bad place') – a vision of a future world gone wrong:

- Aldous Huxley's *Brave New World* (1932) tells of a future society that seems, at first glance, to be fairly pleasant: one might say it's defined by the third of the major rights Thomas Jefferson described in the US Declaration of Independence – 'the pursuit of happiness.' The trouble is that the pursuit of happiness is *all* that defines Huxley's brave new world, which is populated by nihilists who are addicted to sex, drugs, and pleasure but incapable of caring about anyone but themselves.
- George Orwell's *Nineteen Eighty-Four* (1948) is arguably the best of the dystopian novels, and certainly the most famous. In it, the repressed nation of Oceania churns away under the authoritarian rule of an all-powerful government, whose videocameras surveil the lives of every person for possible signs of unacceptable free thought. The posters, broadcasting the phrase 'Big Brother is Watching,' remind every citizen of the cameras recording their lives.
- Margaret Atwood's *The Handmaid's Tale* (1985) tells of a post-nuclear world in which the most radical American religious conservatives have succeeded beyond their wildest expectations, completely subjugating women in the Republic of Gilead to lives of domestic slavery and exiling all who refuse to conform to the deadly 'colonies,' polluted wastelands where few survive.

UTOPIAS AND DYSTOPIAS (cont.)

• Ron Moore's reimagining of the *Battlestar Galactica* television series (2003–9) describes a world in which government arrogance and military secrecy combine to bring about the near-destruction of the human race, and the moral desperation and spartan militarization of humanity's few surviving members.

In most cases, dystopias could function as someone else's utopias. For a true nihilist, *Brave New World* describes a pretty nice place to live – all the pleasure anyone could want. For a true fascist, *Nineteen Eighty-Four* is less frightening – finally, a government powerful enough to maintain national unity. For a true Christian Dominionist, *The Handmaid's Tale* sounds lovely – gender roles enforced once more, and the Bible finally enforced as the rule of life.

Utopias, too, can function as dystopias. It is easy to imagine a version of More's *Utopia* written from the perspective of a slave, or Morris's *News from Nowhere* written from the perspective of survivors of a national disaster (who have no government or major institutions to help them organize recovery efforts), or Skinner's *Walden Two* written from the perspective of someone who feels, on some deep unarticulated level, a longing for personal freedom. Utopias function as utopias only for the people who want them.

Most controversial laws fall into more than one of these three categories. Laws banning abortion, for example, can be justified on the basis of the harm principle (if one considers the embryo or fetus to be a person), the caretaker principle (if one considers abortion to be harmful to the pregnant woman), or the utopian principle (if one considers restrictions on abortion to be an effective way of changing sexual practices). Laws banning hate speech can be justified on the basis of the harm principle (if one believes that hate speech damages its targets), the caretaker principle (if one believes that hate speech damages its speaker), or the utopian principle (if one believes in a society in which hateful ideas are no longer expressed).

Generally speaking, laws that cannot be justified on the basis of the harm principle or the caretaker principle pose an especially potent threat to individual civil liberties. The utopian principle, on its own, is essentially a policymaker's exercise in creativity – allowing the government to shape the behavior of many in order to appeal to the ideals of a few. This is why democracy is usually conducive to civil liberties: because, if nothing else, it makes citizens participants in that creative process.

Civil liberties, human rights, and the two concepts of liberty

If you violate someone's civil liberties, you're also violating that person's human rights. If you violate someone's human rights, you're probably also violating that person's civil liberties. So how do the two ideas differ?

Generally speaking, the differences in the way we use these terms have to do with three factors:

- **Scope**. Civil liberties have to do specifically with liberty (freedom to act) and the ways in which liberty can be repressed. Human rights includes civil liberties, but it also includes issues that generally fall outside of what we think of as constituting them – such as poverty, disease, and homelessness.
- **Emphasis**. While human rights technically includes civil liberties, the additional breadth of human rights as a topic means that relatively small-scale civil liberties violations do not tend to constitute human rights issues. If an employee is fired from a government position for posting compromising photographs on his Facebook account, for example, then

that is an area of concern for civil liberties activists but is unlikely to draw the attention of Amnesty International or the UN Committee on Human Rights.

- **Methodology**. In civil liberties activism, the old adage 'think globally, act locally' applies. But human rights activism relies more on international nongovernment organizations, multinational coalitions, diplomacy, and tribunals, so it tends to encourage more of a 'think globally *and* act globally' approach.

That said, there is considerable overlap between the concepts of human rights and civil liberties and not everyone believes that the two concepts are necessarily distinct. Political historian Isaiah Berlin, in his 1958 essay titled 'Two Concepts of Liberty,' identified two distinct and sometimes competing ideas of liberty: **negative liberty** (or 'freedom from') and **positive liberty** (or 'freedom to'). Negative liberty is freedom from government coercion, or what the framers of the American Declaration of Independence called 'life and liberty,' while positive liberty is the freedom to make livable decisions, or what the framers of the Declaration of Independence called 'the pursuit of happiness.'

Nondiscrimination laws illustrate the tension between the two ideas. According to a pure negative liberty approach, nondiscrimination laws that prevent private businesses from practicing discrimination are wrong because they detract from the freedom that private individuals would otherwise have to discriminate against, or in favor of, anyone they choose. But a broader definition of liberty acknowledges that discrimination reduces the number of live options that people in a discriminated class might have to such an extent that their positive liberty is drastically reduced, which warrants some degree of government intrusion and some specific restrictions on business owners' negative liberty.

A nation operating on the principle of pure negative liberty would have the potential to become as dystopian as any totalitarian government. Without nondiscrimination laws, corporations are free to organize society into castes. Without antitrust laws, monopolies are free to achieve a level of oppressive power that would rival that of any government. Without workers' rights laws, individuals who lack social power can be reduced to slavery. With no social welfare programs of any kind, social mobility becomes impossible, social hierarchies become even more entrenched, and the quality of life for those born into noninfluential families becomes dismal. Such a nation, free though it may be from government intervention, would not be a nation of free people. It would instead be a nation where, to borrow a line from the old Janis Joplin song, 'freedom's just another word for nothin' left to lose.'[1]

But a nation dedicated strictly to positive liberty, with no concept of negative liberty, would be a micromanaged 'nanny state' in which the government claimed the power to ensure equality and happiness in every citizen's life. Since governments are run by the same sorts of human beings that governments are created to protect us from, this never ends well. Equality and happiness according to the Saudi Arabian government, for example, means devout men and submissive women who fully adopt the conservative ideology of Wahhabism. Equality and happiness according to the North Korean government means complete submission to the cult of Kim Jong-il, to whom official government publications attribute supernatural powers and a messianic destiny. Neither government actualizes positive liberty, but both governments are given unfettered power to actualize it. Without negative liberty, such powerful institutions inevitably become corrupt, self-sustaining regimes, the goal of positive liberty ultimately abandoned in favor of destructive utopian ideals.

A nation that is given unlimited power to achieve positive liberty without any real concept of negative liberty is probably much more dangerous than a nation that actualizes negative liberty without any real concept of positive liberty, but compar-

10 'ISMS' YOU NEED TO KNOW

Now that we've defined positive and negative liberty, let's talk about how some common political 'isms' rank on that scale.

Anarchism. The belief that no government is good government. Anarchism is the ultimate expression of negative liberty, but represents no positive liberty. An interesting experiment that, in practice, always disintegrates into despotism because without government, there is nothing to prevent its emergence.

Capitalism. An economic philosophy that emphasizes free markets and relative negative liberty with respect to fiscal issues. Associated with conservatism, libertarianism, and, in the United States, with liberalism as well.

Centrism. A moderate political philosophy, usually represented as a midpoint of some kind between liberalism and conservatism.

Conservatism. A political philosophy that emphasizes negative liberty in fiscal matters, but tends to oppose many forms of positive liberty and to favor more regulation of private behavior than liberalism.

Despotism. Rule of the weak by the strong. The natural form of government, if no alternative form exists.

Fascism. An authoritarian political philosophy marked by extreme nationalism.

Liberalism. A political philosophy that tends to emphasize positive liberty in fiscal matters, and negative liberty with respect to private behavior.

Libertarianism. An offshoot of conservatism favoring negative liberty both with respect to fiscal matters and with respect to private behavior.

Radicalism. The belief that fundamental things need to change in order for the government or social structure to function in a rational way.

Socialism. An economic philosophy that tends to focus on positive liberty and the redistribution of wealth, more or less to the exclusion of negative liberty.

ing the two is equivalent to comparing Dante's eighth circle of Hell with his seventh. Neither are especially pleasant places to live. Both types of liberty play an essential part in what we ordinarily think of as civil liberties or human rights.

The source of liberty

In the next chapter, we'll discuss the origin of the *concept* of rights. But before we go into that, let's take a moment to look at where our rights – those associated with both positive and negative liberty – really come from.

The framers of the eighteenth-century Enlightenment would claim that our rights come from God. In the US Declaration of Independence from Great Britain (1776), for example, Thomas Jefferson referred to natural rights as being 'endowed by [mankind's] creator.' But there are several practical problems with this line of reasoning:

- Governments that protect liberties in the name of God can do other things in the name of God, too. If there is one thing that the horrors of Taliban-led Afghanistan should have taught us, it's that a dangerous precedent is set when leaders believe they are in a position to receive special instructions from God.
- In the increasingly secular and religiously diverse nations of the Western hemisphere, concepts of liberty based on theology are losing their persuasive value – and they never had much persuasive value to begin with for people who did not share at least some elements of the speaker's theology.
- No major world religion focuses in any meaningful way on liberty in the post-Enlightenment sense of the word. As we will discuss in the next chapter, the Hebrew Bible's concept of freedom is collective freedom from foreign occupation,

not personal freedom from the oppression of one's own government.

If rights don't come from God or nature, then it stands to reason that they come from us. But if they don't come from God or nature, how we do know what they are?

What we owe each other

The question of whether civil liberties come from God or nature boil down, essentially, to one question: Are civil liberties brute facts or values? If they are brute facts, then they can be proven, asserted, and demonstrated to any tyrant on Earth. They are fundamental, unchanging, immensely powerful. They apply anywhere and everywhere, just as the laws of physics apply anywhere and everywhere. If civil liberties are brute facts, then everyone who does not respect them denies reality.

But if civil liberties are values, then it becomes impossible to prove that they are worth honoring. Someone who doesn't choose to recognize civil liberties doesn't have to. Any tyrant can dismiss the appeals of civil libertarians simply by expressing disagreement. Values are, if not entirely subjective, communal; in order to share values, people need to share fundamental senti-ments. Arguments about how people should be treated, if they are based on values, fall apart when confronted with someone who honestly doesn't care about the people in question. If someone sincerely believes that anyone not affiliated with his or her religion is an enemy of God and worthy of any torment that can be inflicted, then all the arguments in the world about the value of individual human beings, or the value of love, will fall on deaf ears. And if someone believes that he or she has been given absolute power by God or other fundamental forces of the universe, then no civil liberties argument is likely to chip away at that power.

Politicians, in general, tend to be extremely duplicitous, power-hungry, self-promotional individuals. Politicians who are offered power tend to take it; history is replete with examples of men who were offered absolute power and accepted it, but only a handful of men who were offered absolute power and declined it. The ancient Roman dictator Lucius Quinctius Cincinnatus (519–430 BCE), who had been given absolute control over the Roman Republic very briefly during two crises only to give up that power voluntarily as soon as the crises ended, is often cited as such a figure. George Washington (1732–99), the first US president, was another. In some respects, the final Soviet general secretary Mikhail Gorbachev – who voluntarily reduced the power of his own party, knowing that it could end his administration – was another. But that sort of humility and restraint is very rare. Generally speaking, only the most ambitious and driven politicians achieve significant power – and that ambition, that drive, makes it just as difficult voluntarily to relinquish power, if keeping it is a realistic option.

So it's understandable that we would want to make civil liberties as provably worthwhile as possible. We don't want to rely on the value-systems of political leaders with stunted value-systems. We want to be able to appeal to God or nature or other fundamental principles to show why leaders *must* respect our civil liberties. But they need not. Not unless we force their hand. Thomas Jefferson's Declaration of American Independence is often cited as a perfect summary of the concept of natural rights – but consider the fact that its intended recipient, King George III, did not consider the natural rights argument persuasive. Neither did most of the signers, who were more than willing to ignore the universal concept of inalienable rights with respect to African-American men, all women, nonlandowners, certain foreigners, and others they deemed unworthy.

So if our rights aren't based on provable arguments, what are they, really? To answer that question, let's look at some of the ways we might use the word 'rights' when we're not talking specifically about government policy. We might say, for example, that if I've purchased something, I have a right to keep it. We might say that if I've shoplifted something, I have no right to keep it. We might tell a friend who has been bullied by an employer that he has every right to be angry about it, and that the employer has no right to treat him that way. Can we prove any of this? *Why* do I have a right to keep something I've purchased, but not to keep something I've stolen? *Why* do we have the right to feel angry about being bullied, and why do people in positions of power not have the right to bully others?

Because we say so, and we say so because these are the values we have been inculturated with. These are the values we associate with a meaningful life, the values we associate with a caring life, the values we associate with a respectful life. And they are beautiful values. They are based on moral foundations that, for the most part, we consider basic to who we are.

If we are going to live in a world where commerce means anything, then we have to say that people have the right to keep what they purchase. But if we lived in a world where commerce meant nothing, where private property did not exist, then that right would not exist. If we are going to live in a world where people can keep what they have, then we have to say that people have no right to steal. But if we lived in a world where nobody can own anything, then that right would not exist.

If we are going to live in a world where we say that the strong shouldn't abuse the weak, then we have to say that people have the right to be angry if they're bullied – that it is something that one would be understandably angry about. If indeed we are going to live in a world where we say that the strong shouldn't abuse the weak, then we have to be prepared to say that the strong have no *right* to abuse the weak. But if we lived in a world where it was considered right and just and proper that the strong abuse the weak, if we lived in a world that valued only power, where those who lack power deserve to be treated badly, then the employer would have every right to bully her employee and the employee would have no right to be angry about it.

As I will discuss in the final chapter, our concept of civil liberties – our concept of rights – is based primarily on the habit we have learned to have empathy with, to be concerned about, strangers. But we can't be complacent, because our rights – and the moral values they are based on – exist only because we agree that they do. Orwell's nightmare of a 'boot stamping on a human face forever' is still very real, and civil liberties as fragile as a dried rose pressed between the pages of a book. Our rights exist because we assert them, and we must continue to assert them or they will cease to be.

2
Where did civil liberties come from?

Freedom cannot be bestowed – it must be achieved.

(Elbert Hubbard, *Little Journeys to Homes of the Great*)

The fossil evidence of humanity dates back to at least 130,000 BCE, and cellular analysis suggests that what we call modern humans – members of the species *homo sapiens* – have existed since about 200,000 BCE. We have no evidence of the sorts of societies that humans lived in during most of this time, but looking at isolated, noncitydwelling groups of humans living in more recent times suggests that small groups of people have traditionally picked or been picked by an obvious leader whose counsel they have generally honored. Because these decisions tend to be made at a small-scale, tribal level, this sort of system is more like a family than a government. In some ways this system can be more oppressive, in some ways less, but it is always more intimate and usually not grounded in codified rules or laws.

At some point, these familial tribes began to congregate in cities – most likely because of agriculture, which tends to limit migration. This was the first great, unnatural restriction that civilization imposed on human liberty: It removed the freedom to migrate. As tribes congregated in cities, they were more easily found by other tribes, which would join them and reap the benefits of agriculture and bartering. This transition from a

Figure 3 An Inuit hunter stands over the carcass of a polar bear. For city-dwelling societies, hunting is a sport; in traditional hunter-gatherer societies, it's also the primary source of food.

tribal, migratory hunter-gatherer lifestyle to what we refer to as 'civilization' is believed by most anthropologists to have begun at some point during the past 12,000 years – suggesting that for at least the first ninety-four percent of human history, what we now think of as cities and governments and laws and national identities either did not exist at all, or faded from history without a trace.

When gods ruled the world

The first known civilizations of the ancient world emerged in what we call the Fertile Crescent, stretching from modern-day Egypt in the west to modern-day Turkey in the east. Fed by the Tigris, Euphrates, and Nile rivers, the first of these great empires, called Sumer, began to emerge at some point near 5,000 BCE. For over two millennia, Sumer – occupying the land we now call Iraq – was the dominant empire of the region.

Gilgamesh, whose legend would be chiseled into twelve tablets making up the ancient poem *The Epic of Gilgamesh* is said to have been the great king of Sumer. Described as two-thirds god and one-third human, Gilgamesh was regarded, at least by the author of the *Epic*, as a divine being. The god-king called Pharaoh, ruler of the later Egyptian empire, was also addressed as a supreme being. Throughout the ancient world, governments were grounded in divine authority. To rebel against one's own government was to fight Heaven itself, and to dissent against it was to challenge the word of a living god.

So civil liberties as we know them today weren't crucial issues for governments of the ancient world. More crucial was the power of the king – to protect, to conquer, and to rule.

Divine kings, the church, and the aristocracy

The British–American civil liberties tradition as we have come to know it owes its existence to greedy aristocrats, power-hungry bishops, and megalomaniacal but incompetent monarchs. Were it not for them and their bumbling, blood-soaked centuries of palace intrigue and power-haggling, the concept of natural rights as we know it today might never have developed in Europe or the North American colonies.

So from that vantage point, perhaps the greatest English king of the medieval era was King William II – aka William Rufus – who reigned from 1087 to 1100. Historians contemporaneous to William recorded in *The Anglo-Saxon Chronicle* that he was not easy to get along with:

> He was very rigorous and stern over his land and his men, and towards all his neighbours, and very formidable; and through the counsels of evil men, that were always grateful to him, and

through his own covetousness, he was ever tormenting this nation with an army and with unjust exactions; because in his days every right fell, and every wrong in the sight of God and of the world rose up. God's churches he depressed, and all the bishoprics and abbacies, whose heads died in his days, he either sold for money, or held in his own hand, and let for rent; because he would be the heir of every man, ordained and lay ... And, though I may longer delay it, all that was hateful to God and oppressive to men, all that was customary in this land in his time; and therefore he was hateful to almost all his people.[1]

When he was found dead in 1100 with an arrow in his lung, King William was succeeded by his brother, Henry. It was Henry who gave England its first bill of rights – the Coronation Charter, more commonly known as the Charter of Liberties – which refers to 'unjust exactions' and 'bad customs' under which 'the kingdom of England was unjustly oppressed,' and promises to restrict his own power according to the rule of law.[2] What makes the Charter interesting isn't that it's particularly libertarian – it limits the monarch's oppression of barons and clergy, but says nothing about free speech or privacy or anything of that nature – but rather that it exists at all. The king had historically claimed to *be* the law, by divine right, and here was a king making himself subject to it and limiting the power of his government.

The second and most famous English bill of rights came 115 years later due to the unpopularity of King Henry's grandson, King John. Excommunicated by the Pope and unpopular with barons due to his abuses of power, John signed the Magna Carta ('Great Charter') of 1215 to secure what was left of his power. It didn't do poor John much good, primarily because he came down with a fatal case of dysentery a year later, but the charter is notable for establishing the right of *habeas corpus* and other due process protections.

The 1689 Bill of Rights represented, in a sense, the collision of competing civil liberties interests. The law of Britain at the time was militantly Protestant, so King James II, who had managed to inherit the thrones of England, Scotland and Ireland despite being a Roman Catholic, issued the Declaration of Indulgence of 1687. This was the first significant official statement of religious liberty in British history – as written, it would

Figure 4 A statue of Pope John Paul II overlooks visitors in Mexico City. Although today the leader of the Roman Catholic Church is for the most part a pastoral figure, the Pope ruled over the most powerful dynasties of medieval Europe.

have protected the right to individual religious exercise and banned religious tests. (This was a significant issue at the time, as members of Parliament were required to condemn the Roman Catholic Church before taking office.) When Parliament objected, James dissolved Parliament and established martial law. He was deposed and replaced by the very Protestant King William and Queen Mary, and the 1689 English Bill of Rights was issued to protect the monarch's subjects from oppression.

The 1689 Bill represents a significant evolutionary shift beyond the Charter of Liberties and Magna Carta. It protects freedom of speech in Parliament, bans cruel and unusual punishments, and states that the monarch may not dissolve Parliament, establish new armies, or introduce new taxes without parliamentary approval. Unfortunately, it is also a profoundly anti-Catholic document – declaring, among other things, that no Roman Catholic may serve as monarch. And when it states that citizens have the right to bear arms, it reserves that right for Protestants only.

A tale of two revolutions

The seventeenth and eighteenth centuries represented the golden age of European political philosophy – a period we now refer to as the Enlightenment. Thinkers began to reject the divine right of kings and to believe that they were entitled, by forces more powerful than the government, to civil liberties. Inspired by the overthrow of King James II and the passage of the English Bill of Rights, English philosopher John Locke wrote in the same year:

> A man, as has been proved, cannot subject himself to the arbitrary power of another; and having, in the state of Nature, no arbitrary power over the life, liberty, or possession of another, but only so much as the law of Nature gave him for

the preservation of himself and the rest of mankind, this is all he doth, or can give up to the commonwealth ... Thus the law of Nature stands as an eternal rule to all men, legislators as well as others. The rules that they make for other men's actions must ... be conformable to the law of Nature: i.e., to the will of God, of which that is a declaration, and the fundamental law of Nature being the preservation of mankind, no human sanction can be good or valid against it.[3]

Locke's principle of natural rights dovetailed nicely with the philosophy of fellow British thinker Thomas Hobbes, whose *Leviathan* (1651) posited both natural rights and social contract theory. Hobbes, who famously described pre-social life as 'nasty, brutish, and short,'[4] held that the most fundamental fear was the fear of violent death – and that to escape this, and other fears, people agreed to a social contract.

So by marbling the thought of Hobbes and Locke, one would have a system positing that all people have a natural right to life, liberty, and property, and establish governments to protect this right. Thomas Jefferson, influenced by Hobbes and Locke, did in fact marble these ideas in a context that the two loyal British subjects would have most likely found horrific – the US Declaration of Independence from Great Britain:

We hold these truths to be self-evident, that all men are created equal, that they are endowed by their Creator with certain unalienable Rights, that among these are Life, Liberty and the pursuit of Happiness. – That to secure these rights, Governments are instituted among Men, deriving their just powers from the consent of the governed, – That whenever any Form of Government becomes destructive of these ends, it is the Right of the People to alter or to abolish it, and to insti-tute new Government, laying its foundation on such principles and organizing its powers in such form, as to them shall seem most likely to effect their Safety and Happiness.

In December 2000, the three primary instruments of the European Union agreed to a Charter of Fundamental Rights of the European Union. The treaty, though not yet binding, would be rendered such under both current proposed drafts of the European Constitution. The Charter begins:

> The peoples of Europe, in creating an ever closer union among them, are resolved to share a peaceful future based on common values.
>
> Conscious of its spiritual and moral heritage, the Union is founded on the indivisible, universal values of human dignity, freedom, equality and solidarity; it is based on the principles of democracy and the rule of law. It places the individual at the heart of its activities, by establishing the citizenship of the Union and by creating an area of freedom, security and justice.

While the terminology of the Charter's preamble is different, its basic message is remarkably similar to that of the Declaration of Independence despite the 224-year gap between the two documents; instead of stating that all men are created equal, for example, the Charter states that the universal values of human dignity, freedom, equality, and solidarity will form the basis of the European Union.

Nor are these principles limited by any means to the Western world. The preamble to the 1949 Constitution of India is even more reminiscent of the Declaration of Independence:

> WE, THE PEOPLE OF INDIA, having solemnly resolved to constitute India into a SOVEREIGN SOCIALIST SECULAR DEMOCRATIC REPUBLIC and to secure to all its citizens:
>
> JUSTICE, social, economic and political;
>
> LIBERTY of thought, expression, belief, faith and worship;
>
> EQUALITY of status and of opportunity; and to promote

among them all FRATERNITY assuring the dignity of the
individual and the unity and integrity of the Nation;

IN OUR CONSTITUENT ASSEMBLY this twenty-sixth
day of November, 1949, do HEREBY ADOPT, ENACT
AND GIVE TO OURSELVES THIS CONSTITUTION.

The Constitution of India incorporates not only the 'We the
people' language of Jefferson, but also the 'Liberty, equality,
fraternity!' language that was the rallying cry of the French
Revolution.

The two basic ideas advocated by Hobbes and Locke – the
concept of natural or universal rights, and belief in the social
contract – have defined liberal democracy. It is difficult to
imagine how it can exist without honoring both principles.

Recognizing the implications of both principles is another
matter entirely.

Founders, keepers

Civil liberties have historically been a hypocrite's business. As
we saw above, the Charter of Liberties protected the rights of
clergy and barons but did nothing for the low-class laborers. The
same could be said of the Magna Carta. The English Bill of
Rights extended some rights to the general populace, but specifically denied liberties to Roman Catholics. And the Declaration
of Independence, which declared the equality of all men (but
presumably not women), was written by a white, male, upper-
class slaveowner.

The American Revolution was to a great extent about
smuggling, money, freedom from taxes, and protection from
corrupt government officials. The sweeping language of
Jefferson and other framers aspired to a higher vision of government, but it is a vision of government that has never been fully

actualized – not in the United States, and not anywhere else. The human species has come a long way since the Charter of Liberties, but if the language of Jefferson means anything, it has not come far enough.

Sixteen years after Jefferson declared the equality of all men, but nine years before he would become President of the United States, the British philosopher Mary Wollestonecraft wrote:

> A wild wish has just flown from my heart to my head, and I will not stifle it though it may excite a horse-laugh. I do earnestly wish to see the distinction of sex confounded in society, unless love animates the behaviour. For this distinction is, I am firmly persuaded, the foundation of the weakness of character ascribed to woman; is the cause why the understanding is neglected, whilst accomplishments are acquired with sedulous care: and the same cause accounts for their preferring the graceful before the heroic virtues.[5]

Women did not vote in Britain until 1918, or in the United States until 1920.

William Wells Brown, an escaped African-American slave, wrote his autobiography in 1849. By this point, African-American slavery had already been banned in Britain – but it had not yet been banned in Jefferson's nation, which had ostensibly separated from Britain over the 'all men are created equal' principle. Brown wrote:

> Slavery is a national institution. The nation licenses men to traffic in the bodies and souls of men; it supplies them with public buildings at the capital of the country to keep their victims in. For a paltry sum it gives the auctioneer a license to sell American men, women, and children, upon the auction-stand. The American slave-trader, with the constitution in his hat and his license in his pocket, marches his gang of chained

Figure 5 A London suffragist is arrested at an October 1913 women's rights protest. Although Western post-revolutionary nations began describing themselves as democracies during the eighteenth century, only a minority of the population was actually allowed to vote.

men and women under the very eaves of the nation's capitol. And this, too, in a country professing to be the freest nation in the world. They profess to be democrats, republicans, and to believe in the natural equality of men; that they are 'all created with certain inalienable rights, among which are life, liberty, and the pursuit of happiness.'[6]

Slavery was finally abolished sixteen years after Brown's work went to press. Unlike the majority of slaves in American history, he lived to see it. But it would be another century before state-mandated segregation ended in the American South, and aggregate racial disparities in education, poverty, law-enforcement treatment, legal access, and countless other factors still exist to this day.

The idea of civil liberties is a noble idea, but the history of civil liberties, even in the most progressive of nations, has been one of uncertain progress.

OPEN AND CLOSED SOCIETIES

In his *The Two Sources of Morality and Religion* (1932), French philosopher Henri Bergson defined the concept of open and closed societies. While Bergson identified many characteristics that he associated with these, the primary characteristic of an open society is the free flow of information. Societies that are not open – in which authoritarian leaders control the flow of information – are, by definition, closed.

Today, philosopher and philanthropist George Soros's Open Society Institute (OSI) is dedicated to creating new open societies, preserving and advancing existing open societies, and preventing the formation of closed societies.

The imperial presidency

In May 1977, disgraced former US president Richard M. Nixon was interviewed by BBC journalist David Frost when he dropped a bombshell (emphasis mine):

FROST: 'Would you say there are certain situations ... where the president can decide that it's in the best interests of the nation, and do something illegal?'

NIXON: '*Well, when the president does it, that means it is not illegal.*'

FROST: 'By definition.'

NIXON: 'Exactly, exactly.'[7]

Following revelations that he had aided in the coverup of an illegal June 1972 break-in at Democratic Party headquarters, Nixon resigned in August 1974. But even before the Watergate break-in was public knowledge, and long before Nixon had resigned, concerns had already been raised regarding possible abuses of presidential power. In his 1973 book *The Imperial Presidency*, historian Arthur Schlesinger highlighted the dangers that had already been posed by Nixon's bold assertions of executive power and revelations of secret projects that threatened the integrity of the American democratic system. The January 1970 testimony of a young veteran named Christopher Pyle, who told the country that over 1,500 military intelligence officers had infiltrated liberal activist groups in search of information that could be used by prosecutors or leaked to the press, framed a presidency that still stands as an enduring symbol of arrogant power.

In the years following Nixon's impeachment, Congress and President Jimmy Carter passed a series of reforms intended to reduce the unchecked power of the presidency. Chief among these reforms were the Independent Counsel Act, which established an independent criminal justice agency responsible for investigating the executive branch, and the Foreign Intelligence Surveillance Act (FISA), written to regulate the president's power to conduct 'national security'-related surveillance.

Unfortunately, neither reform was to last. The Office of Independent Counsel expired in 1999 following Independent Counsel Kenneth Starr's many public and lurid investigations into the sexual habits and past financial dealings of President Bill Clinton. Furthermore, the Foreign Intelligence Surveillance Act was openly violated by both Clinton and President George W. Bush – by Clinton in an illegal search conducted against suspected spy Aldrich Ames in 1994, and by Bush in a series of illegal wiretaps conducted against accused terrorists in the years following the September 11, 2001 attacks. In both instances, FISA was revised after the fact to legalize both the president's original violation and, in effect, any similar future violations.

The power of the US presidency is reasserted by every new administration, and there is little indication that legislators of either party have any serious, long-term interest in reducing presidential power. Whether Nixonian power will one day result in future revelations of Nixonian abuses of power remains to be seen, but it is difficult to see this as anything other than an inevitable outcome of an increasingly unregulated presidency.

An emerging European civil liberties framework

The end of World War II left Europe fractured. In its immediate past were the horrors of the Axis Powers, in its immediate future the Iron Curtain and the persistent threat of mutually assured destruction in a global nuclear war. To many, unity appeared to be the only way forward. As Winston Churchill said in a speech to the Academic Youth in Zurich in September 1946:

> [O]ver wide areas a vast quivering mass of tormented, hungry, care-worn and bewildered human beings gape at the ruins of their cities and their homes, and scan the dark horizons for the approach of some new peril, tyranny or terror. Among the victors there is a babel of voices; among the vanquished the sullen silence of despair. That is all that Europeans, grouped in so many ancient states and nations, that is all that the Germanic

races have got by tearing each other to pieces and spreading havoc far and wide. Indeed but for the fact that the great Republic across the Atlantic Ocean has at length realized that the ruin or enslavement of Europe would involve their own fate as well, and has stretched out hands of succor and of guidance, but for that the Dark Ages would have returned in all their cruelty and squalor. Gentlemen, they may still return.

Yet all the while there is a remedy which, if it were generally and spontaneously adopted by the great majority of people in many lands, would as if by a miracle transform the whole scene, and would in a few years make all Europe, or the greater part of it, as free and as happy as Switzerland is to-day. What is this sovereign remedy? It is to re-create the European Family, or as much of it as we can, and to provide it with a structure under which it can dwell in peace, in safety and in freedom. We must build a kind of United States of Europe.

In May 1949, the ten leading powers of Allied Europe signed the Treaty of London and created the Council of Europe. In the years since, European regional unity has become an increasingly realistic goal. The Council of Europe now includes forty-seven member states, and the new European Union – which complements rather than replaces the Council – brings with it the possibility of a single European federal government.

One of the instruments of this unity has been the European Convention on Human Rights, which might seem an odd instrument of unity at first given that human rights are typically a divisive topic. But in Europe, a shared commitment to human rights represented a way of rejecting past mistakes and establishing a clear, shared foundation of fundamental values. These values were put into effect in 1950 through the European Court of Human Rights, responsible for overseeing human rights lawsuits and disputes throughout the territory of the Council of Europe. The Court, which relies on the European Convention

on Human Rights, attempts to enforce protocols that ban
(among other things):

- unlawful detentions,
- unlawful executions,
- torture and degrading treatment,
- slavery and indentured servitude,
- ex post facto laws,
- unnecessary violation of personal privacy,
- laws restricting freedom of expression or religion, unless they
  serve a legitimate public purpose.

While the Court can't impose criminal penalties, it can issue
censures and award monetary damages. And the scope of the
Court is growing. In 1998, Britain passed the Human Rights
Act (HRA), which allows residents to file charges based on the
Convention in British courts without having to deal with the
Council of Europe or press the case in Strasbourg, where the
Court is located (though this remains an option for any residents
who prefer it). The European Union is also scheduled to
adopt the Convention following passage of the Treaty of Lisbon
in 2010.

The International Criminal Court, created in 2002 by treaty,
also serves as a venue for last resort for the prosecution of crimes
against humanity. One hundred and eight nations are currently
signatories to the treaty.

3
Freedom of expression

> No person is your friend (or kin) who demands your silence, or denies your right to grow and be perceived as fully blossomed as you were intended.
>
> (Alice Walker, *In Search of our Mothers' Gardens*)

If knowledge is power, then communication is the basis for democratic power. The right to communicate ideas is fundamental to all democracy; without it, political power is limited to those who are given the privilege of influencing public opinion.

But every government restricts communication in some degree or another. Some speech poses a direct threat to the lives of others and can be legitimately restricted. As US Supreme Court Justice Oliver Wendell Holmes put it in *Schenck v. United States* (1919), 'The most stringent protection of free speech would not protect a man falsely shouting fire in a theater and causing a panic.' Then again, Justice Holmes wrote this famous statement as part of a unanimous ruling supporting the imprisonment of a citizen for speaking out against US participation in World War I. Clearly even the 'shouting fire in a crowded movie theater' standard of dangerous speech can be abused, given a sufficiently broad definition of danger.

So where should the line be drawn?

Dangerous words

The disarming simplicity of the concept of free speech is summed up in the US Constitution's First Amendment, which vows that 'Congress shall make no law ... abridging the freedom of speech, or of the press.' Congress shall make no law, that is, except when it does. Even in the relatively speech-friendly twenty-first-century United States, there are forms of speech that are understandably illegal under the criminal code – most notably threats, speech that disrupts public order, speech that constitutes part of a criminal act, public disclosure of national security secrets, and some forms of obscenity, primarily child pornography. And virtually any kind of speech can be grounds for a civil action if the plaintiff is, or claims to be, harmed by it.

So what does this mean? One thing it doesn't mean is that free speech guarantees are worthless if they're not absolute. After all, it's difficult to imagine calling oneself free in any society where somebody *can* falsely shout 'fire' in a crowded movie theater with impunity – because while citizens of liberal democracies value their right to free speech, they also value their right not to be trampled to death over a mean-spirited prank. 'The Constitution,' US Supreme Court Justice Robert H. Jackson wrote in one 1949 dissenting opinion, 'is not a suicide pact.' But as is true with the Justice Holmes case above, this reasonable-sounding statement was used to back up an argument against free speech rights – in this case, Justice Jackson had written a dissenting opinion in support of a New York law used to restrict public hate speech.

There's nothing particularly sacred about speech that distinguishes it from other actions, other than the fact that it communicates ideas and experiences and that it almost never causes direct harm. But there are times when it can cause indirect harm, and government attempts to protect people from indirectly harmful speech can restrict free speech rights for everyone.

The hate speech debate

TARGETING SKOKIE

The town of Skokie, Illinois boasted a diverse mixture of white, black, and Jewish citizens. Among the city's large Jewish community were an unusual number of elderly Holocaust survivors, who had settled down in this peaceful community to retire.

When the National Socialist (Nazi) Party of America was declined a permit to hold a rally in Chicago's Marquette Park in early 1977, they looked to Skokie as their next venue. The city government reacted in horror – passing a series of city ordinances designed to prevent the Nazis from marching in their town.

In its most unpopular case to date, the American Civil Liberties Union (ACLU) – concerned about the free speech implications of allowing a city to block protesters selectively with new laws – sued the city of Skokie on behalf of the National Socialist Party. In *National Socialist Party of America v. Village of Skokie* (1978), the Supreme Court held that the city ordinances were, in fact, unconstitutional.

Arguing that the original objectives of the rally had been more than met by the national publicity surrounding the case, the Nazi organizers mercifully called off the Skokie march. A year later, they rallied in Marquette Park as originally planned.

Hate speech can be toxic. Not only does it pollute the larger culture with bigotry, potentially having a long-term harmful effect on the lives of those targeted by it, but it also inspires politicians to pass laws criminalizing ideas. It simultaneously threatens vulnerable groups by exploiting our freedoms, and threatens our freedoms by exploiting vulnerable groups. Everyone is harmed in some way by hate speech – including, and sometimes especially, the speaker.

In 2006, the Austrian government sentenced British Holocaust denier David Irving to a three-year sentence for, well, denying the Holocaust. Prior to his arrest in Austria, Irving had achieved international notoriety by filing an unsuccessful libel suit against Holocaust scholar Deborah Lipstadt. In his 2000 ruling on the Irving–Lipstadt case, a British judge rejected Irving's lawsuit – calling him 'an antisemite and a racist' – but up until that point, the case was taken pretty seriously. Such is the reality in much of Western Europe: Speech is threatened by anti-hate speech laws on the one hand, and by broadly written libel laws on the other.

In Britain, it is a criminal offense to 'incite hatred' on the basis of race or religion, and a similar piece of legislation proposed by UK Justice Minister Jack Straw, addressing anti-gay hate speech, is also under consideration. British anti-hate speech laws come with a prison sentence of up to seven years. While the idea of locking bigots in prison is appealing on some level, it's hard to see how laws like these wouldn't have a chilling effect on ordinary speech. Could Richard Dawkins' aggressive critiques of religion, for example, one day run afoul of laws like these? And what would an anti-racial hatred law do to a modern-day Malcolm X, railing in a sometimes fierce way against the injustices of white-dominated culture?

Not that these exceptions are the only concerns. Let's imagine, for the sake of argument, that a public figure were to make a sustained and vigorous argument in favor of racial prejudice that obviously violated UK hate speech laws. Under normal circumstances, that public figure would be seen as a kook and marginalized from public debate – but if arrested and put in prison, that public figure would achieve martyr status. People who might otherwise ignore his or her hateful ideas could give them a second look simply because those hateful ideas had become forbidden fruit. It's human nature to love the underdog, and it's human nature to give credence to silenced opinions.

On the other hand, hate speech does pose a real potential threat to its targets – and people are less likely to spread hateful

Figure 6 A right-wing talk radio host stands in front of an upside-down American flag as he leads a protest against undocumented Latin American immigrants to the United States. In some European nations, harsh rhetoric directed at immigrant communities often runs afoul of laws barring hate speech.

ideas if doing so could lead to a seven-year stretch in prison. In formerly Nazi-occupied Austria, where thinly veiled hate groups still hold considerable political power, banning Holocaust denial makes a certain amount of sense because, if Holocaust denial were to become a commonly expressed opinion, it would stand a very real chance of influencing national culture and national policy.

Civil liberties activists tend to think, and the Western philosophical tradition teaches, that it is much better to respond to hate speech with reason than it is simply to arrest the speakers. From the perspective of civil liberties, letting bigotry make its play for our souls and fail remains the best way to address hate speech. But many who have been victimized by it, and many who have lived in countries that explicitly operated based on it, might understandably find this approach unpersuasive.

And individuals who have been victimized by such countries have every reason to share these apprehensions.

EXCEPTIONS TO FREE SPEECH RIGHTS

Courts have traditionally recognized a variety of exceptions to free speech. Among them:

Public order. The famous 'fire in a crowded theater' example. This can also include speech directed towards provoking a riot, or 'fighting words' intended to provoke a violent reaction from others. Public order is also the basis for banning the public exhibition of material that is offensive to community standards. Speech restrictions on the basis of public order are, as you might imagine, easily abused.

National security. Speech that reveals government secrets to third parties is often considered espionage. As noted later in this chapter, however, a government that is given the unchecked power to restrict speech on the basis of national security will tend to abuse it.

Threats. Death threats are not considered free speech. Neither, quite often, are threats to overthrow the government violently or commit terrorist attacks.

Speech that aids another crime. The words used to commit fraud and extortion, for obvious reasons, are not immune to prosecution.

Pornography. In most countries, at least some forms of pornography are considered outside of free speech protection. Even in the most liberal nations, child pornography is not considered free speech. In the United States, obscene material in general is not considered protected speech as such, though individuals are free to possess it due to privacy rights protections.

Sedition and press freedom

Let's look at the Constitution of North Korea for a moment. Like the Constitutions of most nations founded in the twentieth century, the Constitution of North Korea claims to protect free speech rights: Article 67 promises that every citizen has the right to freedom of speech, press, and assembly. But because the North Korean government has decided that its own stability is of supreme importance, and that an open society would threaten that stability, the North Korean government simply chooses to ignore Article 67. It carries no weight.

North Korea is an extreme example of a country whose leaders value patriotism and ideological cohesion over free speech, but milder examples of this phenomenon can be found in every country on Earth. Take the issue of flag desecration in the United States, for instance. There was little interest in banning the practice until the waning years of the nineteenth century, as ex-Confederates began to prefer the Southern battle flag, the 'stars and bars,' to the official flag of the United States. The anti-flag desecration laws remained in place until the US Supreme Court's ruling in *Texas v. Johnson* (1989), which held that the First Amendment protects symbolic gestures such as flag burning and other forms of flag desecration. Since that time, conservatives in Congress have made seven unsuccessful attempts to amend the US Constitution to prohibit desecration of the flag.

One would be hard pressed to find any government that has not attempted to restrict the speech of its critics at some point or another, because the temptation is always present. When confronted with something that we don't want to hear, all of us might have to resist the urge to shout 'shut up!' or something comparable. If we're especially offended by what we hear, we might even be tempted to respond with physical violence or otherwise behave in an uncharacteristic way. Lawmakers differ from the rest of us only to the extent that they are actually able to silence people. When US President John Adams got tired of hearing challenger Thomas Jefferson's critics refer to him in less-than-respectful terms, he made it illegal to do so. He later lost the election to Jefferson, and the law was repealed, but for a span of several years Adams used his power as president to force his critics to shut up.

And there are also more practical advantages to laws restricting criticism of the government: they allow the government to continue to function without having to deal with public outrage. For governments that are unstable, this can be a particularly strong temptation. In fact, there is almost always a clear inverse proportionality between governments that restrict criticism and stable governments. When a government operates against the wishes of the majority of its citizens, it is always in danger of collapsing. But if dissidents can be silenced by law,

Figure 7 Thousands of Buddhist monks march against the Myanmar military dictatorship of Burma in 2007. Although subjected to arrest and beatings, the monks' actions called further international attention to the crisis.

then other citizens may overestimate the level of support that the government enjoys.

Free speech and national security

Former MI5 agent Peter Wright had retired to Tasmania when he wrote his 1987 memoirs, titled *Spycatcher*. The book was a tell-all autobiography from an industry that was, understandably, less than friendly towards tell-all autobiographies. Wright's stories were particularly troublesome – alleging, among other things, that MI5 agents had set in motion, but then aborted, a plan to destroy the premiership of former prime minister Harold Wilson in 1974 by leaking secret intelligence records profiling Wilson to the press.

The Thatcher administration attempted to block publication and review of Wright's book in Britain – initially with great success. But then things began to unravel. Seven national British newspapers defiantly printed reviews of the book, in violation of the ban. And as controversy ensured international sales, and made black-market copies of the book easily available in Britain, it soon became clear that efforts to restrict the memoirs had failed. In October 1988, Law Lords ruled that *Spycatcher* could be legally printed in Britain – as any damage to national security had already been done.

In the United States, a similar controversy came about during the Vietnam War era. The US Department of Defense had prepared a 14,000-page report titled *United States–Vietnam Relations, 1945–1967*. The inconspicuous-sounding title was attached to a book with explosive implications when excerpts from the document were leaked to *The New York Times* in 1971, revealing (among other things) that President Johnson had lied to the American people about the circumstances surrounding US involvement in Vietnam and escalation of the war. The

Nixon administration attempted to block publication, but the US Supreme Court ruled, in a jumbled 6–3 decision, that the document that became known as *The Pentagon Papers* could, in fact, be freely distributed.

The two cases illustrate the pitfalls of any government policy enacted to restrict free speech on the basis of national security. Few would argue that newspapers be permitted to publish nuclear secrets in a venue where foreign powers could access them, or release confidential advance Secret Service information that could jeopardize the safety of public officials, but what about material that is damaging to national security primarily in the sense that it reveals the existence of practices that rightly embarrass and discredit public officials responsible for making national security decisions?

Porn and indecency

Where laws restricting criticism of the government can be used to hide or shape public opinion, laws against pornography and indecency tend to pander to it. In the United States, broadcast television and radio content is regulated by an indecency standard that appeals specifically to community standards. When Janet Jackson's nipple was exposed during the halftime show at the 2003 Super Bowl, for example, it prompted a wave of radical new broadcast indecency penalties in the United States. Partial nudity is common television fare in much of Europe, but restrictions on broadcast television violence tend to be stricter than in the United States. In Saudi Arabia, standards are even stricter with regard to nudity and sexuality – revealing attire of all kinds is forbidden – but news broadcasts feature more graphic violence than even US audiences would find palatable. In nearly all cases, governments tend to regulate broadcast content based on what audiences would be most likely to find shocking or disgusting.

With respect to Internet content, however, restrictions tend to be much looser in the Western world. In the United States, for example, nearly all pornography with the exception of child pornography is casually distributed online. Laws against the distribution of obscene material exist, but are seldom enforced against pornographic web sites except in extreme cases. When one British Internet proprietor ran a web site selling

Figure 8 A woman wears a burqa while walking down a street in Afghanistan. While many Muslim women choose to wear a burqa, Taliban-controlled Afghanistan made it mandatory – and women who did not comply, or who wore a burqa but violated state ordinances (by speaking to a non-relative male, for example), were subject to severe beatings. In 1998, the Taliban banned women from public hospitals and mandated that the windows in any houses containing women be screened with black ink.

content for coprophilia fetishists, for example, the government shut it down.

The US Congress has made several attempts to ban Internet porn across the board; its first attempt, the Communications Decency Act (CDA) of 1996, would have applied broadcast indecency regulations to the Internet (with heavy fines and prison sentences attached). The law, which would have banned not only pornography but also medical information, public correspondence and literary works containing profanity, and artistic nudity, was ultimately struck down by the US Supreme Court.

Censorship after 9/11

The US political climate immediately following the September 11 terrorist attacks was arguably the most chilling since the Watergate era. When President Bush described the perpetrators of the attacks as 'faceless cowards,'[1] talk show host Bill Maher disagreed with the assessment: 'We have been the cowards, lobbing cruise missiles from 2,000 miles away. That's cowardly. Staying in the airplane when it hits the building, say what you want about it, it's not cowardly.'[2]

White House press secretary Ari Fleischer condemned the remarks when asked about them by a reporter, using language that summed up the chilling effect that fear of terrorism had posed to individual free speech:

> I have not seen the actual transcript of the show itself. But assuming the press reports are right, it's a terrible thing to say, and it's unfortunate. And that's why ... they're reminders to all Americans that they need to watch what they say, watch what they do. This is not a time for remarks like that; there never is.[3]

While the federal government did not take any measures against Maher, his employer – ABC Studios – cancelled his series,

Politically Incorrect with Bill Maher. This was only one of many examples of corporate self-censorship in the wake of the attacks. One somewhat comic example was the distribution, by regional managers at Clear Channel Radio, of an informal list of songs that DJs were advised not to play in the immediate aftermath of the attacks. The inappropriateness of some of the songs at that time, such as Jerry Lee Lewis's 'Great Balls of Fire,' was obvious – but the inclusion of John Lennon's 'Imagine,' Simon and Garfunkel's 'Bridge Over Troubled Waters,' and Louis Armstrong's 'What a Wonderful World' was puzzling.[4] Still, none of this posed a direct threat to civil liberties as such – how corporations use their resources is, in most cases, not a policy issue.

More troubling is what *could* have happened, and what still may in the event of a future terrorist attack. In 2006, former US House Speaker Newt Gingrich delivered what was, coming from the lips a fairly mainstream American politician, a chilling speech:

> And, my prediction to you is that either before we lose a city, or if we are truly stupid, after we lose a city, we will adopt rules of engagement that use every technology we can find to break up their capacity to use the internet, to break up their capacity to use free speech, and to go after people who want to kill us to stop them from recruiting people before they get to reach out and convince young people to destroy their lives while destroying us.[5]

Gingrich does not explain how free speech restrictions would prevent the destruction of a city. He does not explain how the United States would prevent terrorist web sites, most of which are hosted overseas, from being established. He doesn't have to address these sorts of questions, because the fear of losing a city is enough to prevent many people from asking them. At the time Gingrich made his remarks, they were not taken seriously. Had he made them sooner, closer to the September 11 attacks, then they might have brought about a change in policy – in the United States, or in other Western nations.

4

Religious liberty and ideology

> Men never do evil so completely and cheerfully as when they
> do it from religious conviction.
>
> (Blaise Pascal, *Pensées*)

Religious liberty was a pretty big deal for the eighteenth-century Enlightenment thinkers who framed liberal democracy as it is known in the West. Today, it has taken a back seat in the civil liberties debate. While global counterterrorism efforts are sometimes framed in religious terms, most of us have no real concept of what it would be like to live in a culture where warring states, each committed to a particular religious ideology, attempt to eradicate minority faiths on their own soil.

In Europe and the United States, religious liberty is nearly always an issue of conflicting interests. Does the United States' interest in prohibiting the drug trade, for example, prevent religious people from imbibing ceremonial peyote? Does France's interest in promoting integration of new immigrants outweigh a little Muslim girl's right to wear a headscarf to school? These sorts of questions are not always easy to answer.

More stark is what we see of religious oppression in the rest of the world. In China, where being a member of the Falun Gong sect can mean imprisonment, torture, and death; in North Korea, where all religions must be subjugated to the cult of Kim Jong-il; in Saudi Arabia, where criticizing Islam or the Prophet Muhammad is a criminal offense; and everywhere else on Earth where governments take it upon themselves to dictate religious ideology.

What is theocracy?

The word 'theocracy' is tossed around carelessly, which is unfortunate because it stands at risk of being dropped and broken. The Greek root words, *theo-* ('God') and *-cracy* ('rule'), suggest a government actually run by God. When theologians speak of the Theocracy, they are talking about the period of time described in the Hebrew Bible where the Almighty ran things – after Moses received the Ten Commandments, but before the Israelites appointed Saul as their king. That was more or less a theocracy by omission; there was no centralized government, so theologians attribute the nation's relative stability to President God.

This was certainly the sort of government that existed in ancient Egypt, where the Pharaoh functioned as both a king and deity, and there are elements of theocracy in the history of imperial Japan as well. Certainly this was the case in World War II, in which the Emperor Hirohito was understood to be *akitsumikami* ('divinity in human form'). Today, true theocracy is rare; perhaps the only ruler on Earth who claims actually to *be* a god is Kim Jong-il of North Korea, whose government bankrolls an estimated 450,000 'Revolutionary Research Centers' that essentially function as churches. Hymns of praise are sung, and attendees are regaled with stories of Kim Jong-il's allegedly miraculous birth and supernatural powers. What we might call pure theocracy – the idea that the ruler is literally divine and a proper subject of worship – isn't terribly common.

When people use the word today, they generally use it to refer to, for lack of a better term, representative theocracy – a government in which rulers claim to have been elected by God

Figure 9 A portrait of Iranian supreme religious leader Ali Khamenei greets visitors as they arrive at the ruins of Persepolis in the Fars Province of Iran. Khamenei is not an elected leader, but has near-unlimited power in Iran's theocratic government.

to serve, and to have been authorized to act as earthly agents on God's behalf. This is an extremely broad term. Most American presidents have at some time or another described the sense that they were chosen by God to serve, for example, which isn't really an unusual idea – people in general frequently speak of what they think they were 'put on Earth to do,' and some particularly devout folk may go so far as to say that God specifically wanted them to choose the career path that they did. But if the House, Senate, and Supreme Court stated that they agreed with one of these presidents, appointed him president for life, and declared that his words were divine utterances and should be understood to reflect the intentions of God, then that would be a theocracy. Representative theocracy, in other words, is the government *policy* that the ruler has been, or that the rulers have been, chosen by God.

The archetypal example of a representative theocracy is Iran, in which the Ayatollah Khamenei certainly does not claim to be

God but does claim to be God's representative on Earth. The government agrees, and grants him an astonishing amount of power over policy decisions on that basis. Iran has a democratically elected Parliament and prime minister, but it would be impossible for them to overrule the Ayatollah on any issue without rejecting the idea, central to the current structure of the country's government, that he is the medium through which God's wishes are conveyed.

Theocracy – in effect, a merger of government and religion – is the most extreme form of preferentialism. Most views on the relationship between good government and religion can be characterized as preferentialist, accommodationist, or separationist.

THREE PERSPECTIVES ON CHURCH AND STATE

Preferentialism. The philosophy that the government should officially support or endorse a specific religious tradition. We see some of that in Great Britain, where the Church of England enjoys official status, and we see it in most countries of Latin America, where Roman Catholicism is formally endorsed. Generally speaking, this is a fairly harmless preferentialism; the government does not use religion as the basis for an oppressively exhaustive legal code, religious organizations are treated on more-or-less equal terms in court, and religious minorities can operate in peace. There are, however, more troubling forms of preferentialism.

Take the legal system laid out in the Iraqi Constitution of 2005, for example. According to the Constitution's first chapter, Islam is the foundation of Iraqi law and no Iraqi law may contradict the principles of Islam. While the Constitution also guarantees religious freedom and a variety of other civil liberties, the degree to which those protections outweigh the leaders' interpretations of Islam is questionable. Some regimes, such as that of Saudi Arabia, more specifically enforce Islamic law. Conversion from Islam to another faith, for example, is illegal. And the Taliban

THREE PERSPECTIVES ON CHURCH AND STATE (*cont.*)

government of Afghanistan enforced a strict interpretation of Sharia, or Islamic religious law, that essentially confined all women to house arrest under the supervision of male relatives.

Accommodationism. The position that the government should not officially endorse or support any one specific religious tradition, but can offer support to religious organizations as long as it doesn't single any specific religious organization out for exclusive support on the basis of ideology. In the United States, funding of faith-based community service programs and private religious school tuition arguably qualifies as accommodationist. Perhaps the best example of an accommodationist system, however, is that of Israel – which allows claimants to resolve disputes in Jewish, Muslim, or secular courts, as they choose.

Separationism. The idea that the government should not involve itself in religious matters at all. The term itself brings to mind a letter written by US President Thomas Jefferson to the Danbury Baptist Association in 1802, promising a 'wall of separation' between church and state. In practice, pure separationism is difficult to achieve. In 2005, the Osaka High Court of Japan found that Prime Minister Junichiro Koizumi violated the country's church–state separation guarantees by worshiping at the Yasukuni War Shrine while on the clock, and while relying on government-sponsored transportation to and from the shrine. Most forms of separationism are not so strict.

Do religions deserve special status?

England and the United States are struggling with a different problem: Should the government support religious institutions? If so, to what degree? The two countries, with very different religious climates and very different religious histories, are moving along opposite trajectories.

England is, technically speaking, preferentialist. The Church of England has continuously been England's official established church since Queen Elizabeth I made it so in 1558. The United States is, technically speaking, separationist. The Bill of Rights, the ten constitutional amendments ratified in 1789 to protect American civil liberties, begins with the phrase: 'Congress shall make no law respecting an establishment of religion.' The intent of the clause was clearly and specifically written with the idea in mind of avoiding a US counterpart to the Church of England.

And yet the danger of widespread religiously motivated persecution, while relatively low in both countries, could be greater in the more devout United States. Some ninety-four percent of Americans believe in God, and fifty-four percent attend church regularly; in Britain, fifty-five percent believe in God (though sixty-seven percent identify as Christian) and twenty-one percent attend church regularly. While the principle of religious liberty is central to US culture, there are troubling indications that the general public would be amenable to the idea of religious discrimination. Some seventy percent of Americans would support a monument to the Ten Commandments in a government building, for example, but only thirty-three percent would also support the display of a verse from the Qur'an in a government building. Another poll, taken three years after the 9/11 attacks, found that forty-four percent of Americans still supported targeted restrictions on the civil liberties of Muslim Americans. Perhaps most disturbingly, fifty-five percent of Americans believe that the US Constitution, which makes no reference to God or Christianity, establishes the United States as a Christian nation.

On paper, England looks like the sort of Christian nation that many Americans would have in mind. The Queen of England, technically the head of state (a largely symbolic role), holds power to appoint Church of England officials – and the monarch of England may not be Roman Catholic. The Church of England, in turn, benefits from interest on endowments dating back to the sixteenth century, as well as long-unenforced laws prohibiting blasphemy and sacrilege against it. As a matter of policy, England is not only Christian but also Anglican. It has its own official, state-supported church. But that church is, in the words of one church historian, 'in practice disestablished' – no longer part of the English government.[1] Fifty-five percent of members of Parliament would like to make it disestablished in reality, and legislation to accomplish that objective has been under discussion for twenty years. Even the Most Reverend George Carey, former Archbishop of Canterbury and leader of the Church of England, remarked in 2000: 'I expect the Church of England one day to be disestablished.'[2]

Meanwhile, the United States has gravitated towards support of religious institutions. In 1996, President Bill Clinton signed legislation allowing federal funds to be spent in support of religious charities. When President George W. Bush took office in 2001, he created the White House Office of Faith-Based and Community Initiatives to help disperse these funds. It does so at the rate of approximately $2 billion per year. There is also a great deal of popular support for school vouchers, which would allow students who attend the nation's secular public schools to receive federal funds to attend private religious schools if they so choose.

Why is separation of church and state a civil liberties issue?

At face value, church–state separation seems to have more to do with good government than civil liberties as such. It's true that preferentialism and accommodationism need not pose any direct threat to the civil liberties of citizens, and that it is entirely possible, in principle, to have a civil libertarian government that has a religious establishment. The United Kingdom is an excellent example.

But in most instances where church and state lines are blurred today, it is because a religious agenda has become so dominant in a given country that it needs to be given an officially dominant role in public policy as well. This is dangerous for a variety of reasons. Among them:

1. For a devout believer, religion can be more important than anything – including civil liberties and quality of life. A government that has an official religion is a government that can do anything in the name of religion.
2. Most religions suggest legal codes that violate civil liberties. For example, a literalistic interpretation of the ancient Mosaic code would require people to be stoned to death for blasphemy, and even children to be stoned to death for cursing their parents. If a government claims to adhere to the principles of a specific religion, then it is opening up the possibility of enforcing that religion's mandates by law. (Though religiously motivated legislation is by no means limited to countries that officially acknowledge one religion over others.)
3. Government support of one religion relegates members of all other faiths to second-class citizenship status. If the town church is paid for but the town mosque is not, then Muslim citizens already face significant discrimination even if that is the only effect of a religious establishment. This in turn opens the door to more severe forms of discrimination and oppression.

But religious discrimination is almost never grounded *entirely* in religious motives.

Oppression and assimilation

All religions operate under a cloud of potential oppression in China, but it is those religious organizations that the government has classified as 'heretical' that face the most persistent threat. And no 'heretical' religious movement has faced more severe treatment at the hands of the Chinese government in recent years than the very new, very Chinese spiritual tradition of Falun Gong.

Founded in 1992 by Li Hongzi, Falun Gong is one of many *qi gong* traditions emphasizing the cultivation of *qi*, or spiritual power. Adherents of Falun Gong learn four standing meditative techniques and one sitting meditative technique, all of which are generally practiced outdoors. Falun Gong also encourages traditional Chinese naturopathy, a trait that the Chinese government has generally welcomed given the considerable strain under which the national health care system operates.

Over time, however, Falun Gong simply got too big. According to a 1994 report by the Chinese government, there were over seventy million Falun Gong adherents in China. There are also, not coincidentally, approximately seventy million voluntary members of the Communist Party of China. During Mao Tse-tung's Cultural Revolution of 1966, 'superstitious' traditions were seen as dangerous and attempts were made to stamp them out in the name of promoting a more contemporary, scientific, and socialist worldview. As Falun Gong and similar, but smaller, traditions began to attract vast numbers of followers, the government began cracking down on the tradition. Falun Gong is officially banned in China, with proponents subjected to imprisonment, beatings, and torture. In a 2000 report, Amnesty International stated that '[a]ll the information available indicates that the crackdown is politically motivated.'[3]

Most instances of religious oppression do in fact appear to be politically motivated, at least on some level. When Saudi Arabia

Figure 10 A member of China's Falun Gong sect demonstrates a torture technique used by the Chinese government against dissidents as part of a human rights protest.

marginalizes Shiite Muslims from its society, for example, it achieves both the religious objective of ideological purity and the political objective of limiting the presence and influence of those who might not support the political status quo. Most severe forms of oppression serve the primary or secondary purpose of ensuring that the regime in power remains in power, and is not challenged by dissenting minority groups.

A more benign way to decrease the size of dissenting minority groups is to enact milder policies with the goal of reeducation or assimilation. In 2004, for example, popular fear of growing Islamic influence led French legislators to ban girls from wearing headscarves in the nation's public school system. This seemingly arbitrary act serves several practical purposes:

1. It makes Muslim girls in French public schools feel less out of place, as their manner of dress is closer to that of their French peers;

2. It forces parents to choose between French values and the values of traditionally Islamic cultures – essentially putting them in a position where they must decide whether or not they intend to participate in mainstream French culture;

3. It marginalizes the most conservative Muslim families from the mainstream of French society, reducing their ability to influence national culture; and

4. It discourages the most conservative Muslim families from immigrating to France.

It also stands the risk of backfiring, however. If the number of conservative families approaches or exceeds the number of families willing to participate in the secular public school system, then an entire generation of French children will be raised in a relatively isolated conservative Islamic culture within France. This would obviously run counter to the intended goal of cultural assimilation. These sorts of policies also tend to generate hostility against the government and mainstream culture, which is obviously not conducive to assimilation.

And it is difficult to argue that this sort of targeted restriction on religious freedom does not pose a human rights problem. Certainly the preservation of secular culture is essential to the preservation of civil liberties as we currently know them, but the violation of civil liberties in the short term does not augur well for this long-term goal.

Blasphemy and apostasy

When religious freedom is threatened, the government asserts an illegitimate power: the power to dictate the thoughts and opinions of its citizens. Freedom of speech protects the expression of ideas – but the power to *hold* contrary ideas begins with religious freedom. The importance of this is lost on many

Westerners, who take it for granted that the government lacks the authority to regulate their thoughts, but there was a time when this was seen as part of the government's mandate. In 380 CE, the Roman emperor Valerian decreed:

> We will that all our subjects ... believe the one divinity of the Father, Son and Holy Spirit, of majesty co-equal, in the holy Trinity. We will that all those who embrace this creed be called Catholic Christians. We brand all the senseless followers of other religions by the infamous name of heretics, and forbid their conventicles to assume the name of churches.[4]

Blasphemy, later known as blasphemous libel, was illegal in England and Wales until May 2008. The last application of the law, the 1977 prosecution of *Gay News* editor Denis Lemon, had as much to do with homophobia as it did with religion. He was fined, and given a nine-month suspended sentence, for publishing James Kirkup's erotic poem titled 'The Love That Dares to Speak Its Name,' which invents a sexual relationship between Jesus and the centurion who stabbed him with a spear. Following Jesus's removal from the cross, the poem goes, the centurion performed sexual acts on him. (Although it is often described as promoting necrophilia, this is not entirely accurate; in the poem, Jesus was clearly alive, albeit barely alive, at the time he was removed from the cross.) But more offensive than the sex scene itself, from the perspective of blasphemous libel, was the assertion that Jesus was a gay man, and 'had it off with other men,' including Pontius Pilate, John the Baptist, and all twelve disciples.

While blasphemous libel laws have fallen out of favor in Europe, laws prohibiting hate speech – discussed in chapter 3 – overlap with laws restricting blasphemous libel. Between 1997 and 2008, for example, Brigitte Bardot was fined five times under French hate crime laws for making anti-Muslim remarks.[5]

It is conceivable that a poem such as Kirkup's, which ran afoul of blasphemous libel law decades ago, could one day run afoul of religious anti-hate speech laws based on an argument that it disparages a religious faith. But there is a key difference between blasphemous libel laws, as they are generally constructed, and hate speech laws: Blasphemous libel laws are nearly always preferentialist, written to protect one religion, while hate speech laws are accommodationist, written to protect all religions.

This is a significant distinction, given that blasphemy itself remains illegal in much of the world – and sometimes with penalties far worse than those seen in Europe in the modern era. In April 2008, Sabri Bogday was sentenced to death by the Saudi Arabian government for using God's name in vain during an argument with a neighbor.[6] At the time of writing, he remains on death row. In Pakistan, Dr. Mohammed Younas Sheikh was sentenced to death for blasphemy in 2002, then finally acquitted on appeal and released in late 2003 – no doubt in part because he never actually made the remarks he had been accused of making. As Sheikh wrote after his release:

> The charges against me centred on some utterances I was alleged to have made in the course of a lecture at the college on 2nd October 2000, that neither the Prophet of Islam nor his parents could have been Muslims before Islam was revealed to the Prophet. I was also alleged to have said that the Prophet was unlikely to have shaved under his armpits since the custom was probably unknown to his tribe at the time. These remarks were interpreted by my accusers, the Mullahs, as an insult to the Prophet. I did not actually make the alleged remarks. The mullahs themselves never heard me make any such remarks, nor did they investigate whether any such incident had ever occurred. In fact, I gave no lecture at the time alleged ...
>
> The retrial was held in November 2003 at the Court of the Session in Islamabad. Because of threats and harassment no

lawyer was ready to plead my case, and I was forced to defend myself for survival, which I did after secretly smuggling law books into my death cell ... The judge accepted my legal arguments and found charges against me baseless. My accusers, the two Mullahs and the Islamist students had lied under oath.

I was acquitted on 21st November 2003.[7]

In much of the Middle East, apostasy – conversion from Islam to another religion – is also a capital offense. But many were surprised when the postinvasion government of Afghanistan, still operating under US and allied protection, sentenced Abdul Rahman to death in February 2006 for converting from Islam to Christianity. As was the case with Mohammed Younas Sheikh, he was eventually released on a technicality – leaving the death penalty intact in Afghanistan as the nation's official punishment for apostasy. Fearing vigilantes, Rahman fled Afghanistan and is currently living in Italy.[8]

The new fundamentalism

In the 1960s, as Egyptian president Gamal Abdel Nasser pushed forward reforms to modernize his country and make it a more inclusive nation, he ran afoul of Sharia hardliners who called for a strict imposition of Islamic law. The most influential of these hardliners was author and activist Sayyid Qutb, leader of Egypt's Muslim Brotherhood. In his three works, which included two volumes of theology and a commentary on the Qur'an, Qutb argued that Muslim nations had become too lax in cracking down on non-Muslims and secular Muslims. Nasser's philosophy of Islamic modernism became known as Nasserism; Qutb's philosophy of strict, repressive Islamism and radical opposition to moderate Islamic governments as Qutbism. Qutb, executed in 1966 for allegedly masterminding an attempted assassination plot against Nasser, soon became both a martyr and the most famous Islamic fundamentalist thinker of the twentieth century. His philosophy would later function as the ideological cornerstone for al-Qaeda and most other international Islamic terrorist groups.

Christianity offers its own answer to Qutbism in the Christian Reconstructionism movement of the late American theologian R.J. Rushdoony. Rushdoony argued that the Bible commands Christians to dominate secular and moderate Christian governments and replace them with governments in which biblical law would reign supreme. There is no room in Rushdoony's model for modern liberal democracy. 'Democracy,' he wrote, 'is the great love of the failures and cowards of life.' Like Qutb, Rushdoony mandated public executions for private and victimless offenses against religious sensibilities, such as blasphemy and homosexuality. Rushdoony was also a white supremacist and eugenicist who denied the Holocaust, supported racial segregation, praised 'selective breeding' as a means of eliminating 'defective persons,' used racial epithets, and defended past enslavement of African-Americans (though he claimed that '[o]nly a minority of the slaves ever worked'). While Rushdoony never achieved anything approaching Qutb's level of influence, the organization he founded – called the Chalcedon Foundation – remains active.

5

In the name of the law

It is wrong to think that belief in freedom always leads to victory; we must always be prepared for it to lead to defeat. If we choose freedom, then we must be prepared to perish along with it.

(Karl Popper, *All Life is Problem Solving*)

The most fundamental right, in the Western tradition of liberal democracy, is essentially the right to be left alone. We see this right manifested in different ways – in protection from unwarranted searches, for example, or in the freedom to speak or worship as one likes – but what it all generally boils down to is the right to live our own lives as we see fit and, as long as we're not hurting anybody, to do so without having to worry about being arrested, fined, supervised, or harassed by government officials.

Governments interfere with this right fairly regularly. Sometimes they do it to pander to public opinion. Sometimes they do it to expand their political power. But most of the time, they do it out of fear of crime and terrorism.

Live on camera

In his 1948 novel *Nineteen Eighty-Four*, British writer and journalist George Orwell expressed contagious fear of a regime in which all people were completely monitored and the actions of the government completely hidden, where dissent was illegal and change impossible – a regime that represented 'a boot stamping on a human face forever.' Sixty years after Orwell's novel was published, the fascist and Stalinist bogeymen who inspired it have long since left the political scene – but the technology that would make such a society possible has been invented, and is gradually becoming inexpensive enough to put into use.

London, for example, is overseen by a 'surveillance veil' of 10,000 closed-circuit security cameras mounted throughout the city. If it happens outdoors in London, odds are good that it happens on camera. New York City is in the process of implementing a similar but less ambitious plan; by 2010, over 3,000 cameras will monitor city activity. The hope is that the cameras will reduce crime and terrorism, or at least make it more possible to prosecute serious offenses after the fact.

But no country symbolizes the power and dangers of the surveillance state more than China, and no city symbolizes the excesses of the Chinese surveillance state more than the Shenzhen special economic zone. As human rights activist Naomi Klein explains:

[By 2008] some 200,000 surveillance cameras [had] been installed throughout the city. Many are in public spaces, disguised as lampposts. The closed-circuit TV cameras will soon be connected to a single, nationwide network, an all-seeing system that will be capable of tracking and identifying anyone who comes within its range – a project driven in part by U.S. technology and investment. Over the next three years, Chinese security executives predict they will install as many as 2 million CCTVs in Shenzhen, which would make it the most watched city in the world.[1]

Figure 11 Surveillance cameras monitor foot traffic in Madrid.

Given Shenzhen's population of 12.4 million, that would work out to one camera for every six residents or so.

Small towns are also beginning to experience the surveillance boom. City officials in Dillingham, Alaska (population 2,400) were able to acquire a $202,000 grant from the US Department of Homeland Security to install eighty security cameras throughout the town. That's one camera for every thirty people. As camera technology becomes less expensive, it's only a matter of time before cities can afford to buy a camera for every fifteen people, or every five people, or one camera per person. The implications for personal privacy are considerable.

In August 2007, Misumi Electronics Corporation announced the MO-R803 – a fully functional cylindrical digital camera less than an inch long and less than one-fifth of an inch in diameter – billing it the 'world's smallest camera.' Microcameras have already proven useful in medicine – some physicians have replaced traditional colonoscopies with 'mouth-to-anus endoscopy,' in which the patient simply swallows and passes a camera pill – but it's not difficult to imagine tiny cameras of this kind being used for covert surveillance.

WATCHING THE WATCHMEN

While the future of surveillance is frightening, the past and present aren't always exactly comforting, either. The list of government surveillance programs, even in Western liberal democracies, is very long. Among the more infamous:

- **COINTELPRO.** A long-term surveillance program operated by the US Federal Bureau of Investigation from 1956 to 1971. Officers would infiltrate civil rights organizations and other alleged subversive groups and report on their findings, which often included surveillance of public figures such as Martin Luther King Jr.
- **ECHELON.** A joint project of the Australian, Canadian, New Zealand, UK, and US governments that intercepts satellite signals and other wireless communications using radar domes and other equipment. Has been in continuous operation since 1947. The scope of the project is unknown, but it may have the power to intercept telephone calls and email messages, among other things.
- **Total Information Awareness (TIA).** A program of the US

WATCHING THE WATCHMEN (*cont.*)

Department of Defense that was originally designed to create a massive database of all citizens and possibly those outside of the United States as well, linking all of them to various activities and interests by the use of data mining. Created in 2002, but was de-funded and dismantled in 2003 following public outcry.

- **Terrorist Surveillance Program (TSP).** An illegal program conducted by the US National Security Administration to spy on telephone conversations between US and international parties without search warrants, in violation of the Federal Intelligence Surveillance Act (FISA). In 2008, the law was revised to accommodate wider surveillance of international telephone calls, effectively legalizing the program.

And if tiny cameras on Earth aren't sufficiently problematic, think about the possibilities presented by massive cameras mounted on airplanes and satellites. Google, through its Google Maps and Google Earth services, has captured people sunbathing on their roofs in various stages of undress and men urinating behind bushes along the side of the road. Between the cameras far above, surveillance cameras mounted above streets and subways, and tiny spy cameras that can be hidden virtually anywhere, it's difficult to imagine how privacy can be protected in the twenty-first century. And the cameras above are only becoming sharper, the surveillance cameras more plentiful, the spy cameras cheaper and smaller. Orwell's vision of a supervised society seems not only plausible, but easily plausible. So what protects us from it?

In most modern constitutional democracies, there is a legal distinction made between private and public spaces. Surveilling public spaces, in legal terms, is nothing special; governments can generally do so without a warrant. But surveilling private spaces generally requires a search warrant; it's not something that most governments can implement on a widespread basis as a preventative measure, and as long as individual citizens value their privacy, this is unlikely to change.

Governments are also subject to surveillance in their own right. The March 1991 beating of Rodney King was captured on videotape because a witness, George Holliday, had received a home videocamera for Christmas. Now digital cameras come with most industry-standard cell phones, and citizens use these digital cameras to document civil liberties abuses – uploading video recordings of the abuses to video-sharing sites such as YouTube. Just as new technology permits the government to monitor citizens, it also permits citizens to monitor governments more effectively. When officers of the infamous Los Angeles Police Department attacked Latino protesters at a May 2007 immigration rally in MacArthur Park, they also beat journalists covering the event and attempted to destroy their cameras. Unfortunately for the officers, their destruction of journalists' cameras was captured on film by other cameras. Goverments, like the private citizens under their jurisdiction, are unable to escape the implications of video surveillance.

The tools of self-defense

CIVIL LIBERTIES AND SMALL GOVERNMENT

Between 1838 and 1851, *The United States Magazine and Democratic Review* was a crucial venue in the US public policy debate. Its motto, 'That government is best which governs least,' represented the New England spirit of local autonomy and limited regulation. If one supported local governments while limiting the power of the national government, the theory went, then personal liberties would most likely remain protected. The US debate over slavery would test this idea.

CIVIL LIBERTIES AND SMALL GOVERNMENT (*cont.*)

The federal government banned the international slave trade in 1808, but left domestic slavery as a question to be resolved at the local level. The presumption from abolitionists of the time was most likely that after the international slave trade was eliminated, domestic slavery would be abolished, state by state. What early abolitionists did not count on was the possibility that entire Southern agricultural economies would be built around the unpaid labor that slavery provided – to the point where they would not have functioned without that unpaid labor.

Southern legislatures not only supported slavery, but took additional measures to keep it in place. In South Carolina, it was essentially legal to kill one's own slave (the law against it was seldom enforced) but illegal to teach a slave to read and write. The issue of fugitive slaves was even more of a sticking point – with many slaves fleeing to Northern states for sanctuary, and Southern legislatures insisting that federal legislation be passed to prevent them from having it.[2] That legislation came in the form of the Fugitive Slave Act of 1850, but as Northern states refused to co-operate with it, Southern politicians began to raise the idea of secession – and, with it, the inevitability of civil war. When the Fourteenth Amendment was ratified after the war, it sent the message that personal civil liberties would no longer be left to the discretion of the states.

The issue of slavery had made it clear that local autonomy was no longer a reliable principle in protecting individual liberty, because local autonomy had left millions of Americans enslaved for generations. By leaving the issue of racial segregation to the states for almost a century to come, the US government continued to leave intact 'Jim Crow' laws upholding the racial caste system in which the institution of slavery was grounded. Today, the principle of local autonomy is used to justify legislation restricting the rights of many identifiable groups living in the United States, from undocumented immigrants to lesbians and gay men.

In eighteenth-century North America, revolutionaries didn't have cameras but they did have rifles. They turned against the British Empire by force, which reluctantly backed away and allowed them to become an independent nation. Then, as now, the threat of violent force is a deterrent to oppressive government. It isn't a difficult idea to grasp: In any disagreement in which two people are armed, and one person drops the weapon, the person who remains armed holds a considerable tactical advantage. Defenders of the Second Amendment to the US Constitution, which protects 'the right of the people to keep and bear Arms,' often cite this deterrent effect when defending their right to carry firearms. If citizens are unarmed, the argument goes, then a government can oppress them by force without finding itself in a real war.

But much like surveillance technology, weapon technology has improved over the centuries. The powder-loaded muskets of

Figure 12 A certificate stating membership in a US citizen militia, *c.* 1805. The United States was founded with an armed citizenry and no professional army; many of the founders preferred to rely on their own guns for self-defense, and considered a professional army to be an invitation to tyranny. From this attitude came the Second Amendment to the US Constitution, protecting the right to keep and bear arms.

the American revolutionary era, which fired only a single shot at a time, barely qualify as weapons when compared with state-of-the-art high-caliber semiautomatic rifles. Handguns can be easily concealed, then whipped out at a moment's notice with deadly consequences. The tools have changed. Should Americans' way of thinking about weapons change with them?

In Britain, against whom the United States developed its doctrine of the right to bear arms, the context of the gun control debate is very different. While the 1689 Bill of Rights theoretically protects the right of citizens to own weapons for self-defense, there is little sense on the eastern side of the Atlantic that citizens should want to arm themselves to discourage government oppression. Arguments regarding gun ownership tend to focus on more practical concerns – namely, should citizens use guns to protect themselves against crime? The answer has generally been no, leading to some of the most restrictive gun ownership policies of any democratic nation on Earth.

Gun rights is not often described as a civil liberties issue, and in some respects the way the debate has been framed is not conducive to civil liberties sensibilities. Take the debate over self-defense for crime victims, for example. In Britain, the law strongly discourages citizens from taking matters into their own hands. When one English citizen used a toy gun to capture burglars, he was arrested for it. When another shot a robber, he was sentenced to life in prison. In most contexts in the United States, a citizen confronting robbers in his or her own home can legally shoot them without having to worry as much about criminal penalties. In this sort of situation there are actually two civil liberties concerns at work – the victim's right to self-defense, and the burglar's right to equal protection under the law. One or the other must be sacrificed. In deciding whether citizens may use deadly force to protect themselves and their property, governments must decide whether to mandate passive victimhood or deputize vigilantism. Neither option is particularly appealing, but there is no third choice.

With respect to the issue of firearm ownership itself, however, there is a clearer civil liberties connection. Whatever the effects of large-scale firearm ownership on the crime rate, it is difficult to make the argument that a well-armed population is not an effective deterrent to government oppression.

WARS FOR, AND ON, DRUGS

Bans on recreational drugs were relatively rare until the modern era. The seventh-century BCE Greek legal codes of Draco and Zaleucus are purported to ban the consumption of undiluted wine,[3] and some of the more conservative Islamic legal traditions have banned alcohol (and coffee) intermittently since the late seventh century CE, but such pre-nineteenth-century regulations are relatively rare.

In the First Opium War (1839–42), the government of Britain even went so far as to declare war on China in hopes of forcing the Chinese government to import British opium. The latter had made several attempts to end the trade, but was ultimately forced to permit British opium imports as a condition of the treaty ending the war. Britain would go on to ban heroin, an opium derivative, in 1920.

In the United States, the 'War on Drugs' – a concept that originated with President Dwight D. Eisenhower in the early 1950s – has become one of the most significant law enforcement failures in US history.

Under arrest

Thomas Jefferson's Declaration of Independence refers to inalienable rights to life, liberty, and the pursuit of happiness, but the reality is that all three rights are alienable in most nations.

Governments deprive citizens of life through capital punishment (more on that later), and arrest and imprisonment deprive citizens of liberty and the pursuit of happiness.

There are mechanisms that most liberal systems of criminal justice have implemented to prevent law enforcement abuse. Although these mechanisms are not completely foolproof, they provide an essential bare minimum level of protection. They are:

- *Habeas corpus* ('you have the body'), the right of any prisoner to challenge the terms of his or her arrest before an impartial judge.
- Right to equal counsel, as modern criminal justice systems are so procedurally complicated that only an attorney can provide adequate defense.
- Right to protection from torture (discussed below), police brutality, and other forms of coercion.

All three of these mechanisms have been asserted, repeatedly, in UN human rights conventions. In practice, however, these mechanisms are not always honored by signatory nations – even by liberal democracies that tout their human rights record. The United States, for example, arrested and detained 775 nonUS prisoners at the Guantanamo Bay military base in Cuba, with no *habeas corpus* protection and inadequate access to counsel, in the years following the September 11, 2001 terrorist attacks. Some former prisoners also report that torture was used against them, and the US government has admitted to the use of some non-lethal torture techniques (often called 'torture-lite' or 'moderate physical pressure') as part of its post-9/11 detention program.

And in countries that are not liberal democracies, and do not pretend to be, the situation is far more dire. Countries that cannot afford to maintain, and/or are not challenged to maintain, a useful appeals system essentially allow agents of local

Figure 13 An ACLU member protests the US government's post-9/11 'enemy combatant' policies, which deprived suspected terrorists of their *habeas corpus* rights.

government to exercise unchecked power over the citizens under their jurisdiction.

Behind bars

Until the past few centuries, prisons weren't commonly used. Criminals would be subject to fines, slavery, torture, public humiliation, death, and mutilation of the corpse – but they wouldn't generally be sentenced to hard time in prison, because there weren't many prisons to hold them yet. Jails and dungeons were used, but most often only as places to house prisoners awaiting their punishments.

It was not until the early nineteenth century that the *penitentiary* system – which was intended, literally, to be a system that creates penitents – was developed. Over time, it has become the gold standard of punishment. In most Western democracies, serious offenses are most often punished by prison time. Compared to older methods of punishment, prisons seem fairly humane – they keep offenders separated from the general population so they can't offend again, they are administered (at least in theory) with the objective of rehabilitating the prisoners, and they can accomplish these objectives without killing or physically torturing prisoners.

But prisons aren't always as humane as they might initially appear, prisoners aren't always guilty of the offenses with which they have been charged, and sometimes, practical concerns such as rehabilitation and protection of the general public take a back

Figure 14 Illustration depicting Walnut Street Prison in Philadelphia, Pennsylvania, which was founded in 1790 by Quakers as the first modern penitentiary.

seat to less savory motivations such as fear, social engineering, and revenge.

When historians look back on the United States of the twentieth and twenty-first centuries, they will most likely notice that its government did some things exceptionally well. It established the most powerful and affluent economy on Earth, the most technologically advanced military on Earth, and it was among the first governments to extend suffrage to members of both sexes, and ... it imprisoned more people than any other country on Earth.

The United States comprises only five percent of the global population, but the country's 2.3 million prisoners make up twenty-five percent of the global prison population. The rate of incarceration varies – Latinos are three times more likely to be incarcerated, on average, than whites; African-Americans, more than six times as likely.[4] For comparative purposes, we can look at the government of Britain – where the prison population of England and Wales has recently peaked at 77,000.[5]

Aryeh Neier, former executive director of the American Civil Liberties Union (ACLU) and co-founder of Human Rights Watch, argues that 'the most important violations of [US] civil liberties of the past two decades' are 'the steady deterioration in the quality of legal counsel provided by the states to indigent criminal defendants' and 'the incarceration of 2 million Americans at a time and tens of millions over the course of a lifetime.'[6] Poverty and imprisonment have a cyclical relationship with each other; poverty, in addition to creating crime on its own merits, also limits access to adequate defense counsel – thus increasing the risk of incarceration. Incarceration, in turn, removes convicts from the workforce and contributes to poverty. There is also some doubt as to the efficacy of US prisons; more than half of prisoners released from prison are sent back within three years due to new offenses or parole violations.[7]

One new approach to addressing the problems of high incarceration and recidivism is the community court system, in which nonviolent offenders are dealt with in local courts, sentenced to local community service, and given access to vocational training, counseling, and other rehabilitative tools. The New York State Drug Court, for example, requires graduates of its rehabilitation program to be clean and sober for a minimum amount of time, commit no new offenses, pass the GED or otherwise obtain a high school diploma, take employment training, perform community service, and be either employed or attending college at the time of program completion. Furthermore, graduates continue to receive supervision and counseling on a long-term basis after completing the program. In the Bronx program, only five percent of program graduates were arrested for another offense within two years.[8]

Torture and abuse

It's difficult to know how common torture is, because it is by definition something that governments don't publicize or keep records about, but the cases are not scattered and isolated. A 2006 study conducted by the Boston Medical Center found that eleven percent of foreign-born visitors to the primary care clinic reported that they had been tortured before they emigrated to the United States.[9] Taking into account the facts that emigrating to the United States is not an option for most victims of torture, that the United States receives a disproportionately high percentage of foreign-born immigrants from countries where torture is uncommon, that some victims of torture would be reticent to report their experiences in a survey, and that torture in US prisons is not unheard of, the global percentage of torture survivors is most likely higher than the reported eleven percent.

Because reliable data on the matter is not available, however, all such estimates are bound to be speculative to some degree. International human rights groups prefer to focus on known, specific instances of torture, preferably representing cases where evidence is available to support the torture claim – cases that, by their very existence, reveal broader patterns of torture and indict the governments responsible. Amnesty International's 2008 report, for example, describes the following cases:

- China, generally regarded as one of the most prolific torture regimes on Earth, targets civil liberties activists. Farm workers' rights activist Yang Chunlin, for example, has been arrested and tortured on numerous occasions. One method favored by Chinese police has been to tie his arms and legs to a four-post bed, in the manner of a medieval rack, and then leave him hanging in that position for days at a time.
- In Egypt, to whom US international prisoners are frequently outsourced for torture, it is a reality of prison life. Thirteen-year-old Mohamed Mamduh Abdel Rahman was tortured to death in August 2007 for allegedly stealing packets of tea.
- In Eritrea, dissidents are routinely hog-tied and hung by the wrists and feet from a tree limb by police in a form of torture known as 'the helicopter.'
- In Kenya, police searching for a teacher known for his human rights activism found his wife, Mary Muragwa, alone at his house. They arrested her, subjecting her to beatings, rape, and other forms of torture for four months in hopes of drawing information on her husband's whereabouts.

Again, these should not be regarded as isolated cases – because most torture victims, for obvious reasons, are not likely to risk further torture or death by reporting their experiences to international human rights groups. They are, instead, representative of broader patterns.

Although UN human rights conventions prohibit the use of torture, these conventions are not enforced. In fact, China and Egypt are current members of the UN Human Rights Council – and China, Egypt, Eritrea, and Kenya were all members of the UN Commission on Human Rights in 2005, the last year of its operation.

US TORTURE AFTER 9/11

In November 2005, US President George W. Bush said something bold, stunning, and completely false: 'The United States of America does not torture. And that's important for people around the world to understand.'[10] It's true that the United States no longer tortures as a matter of *policy*, but – like virtually all nations – it occasionally practices torture, and has done so since its inception. One 1672 Massachusetts law, for example, specifically authorizes the use of torture in cases where one suspect has been apprehended and the names of conspirators are sought.[11] And when President Theodore Roosevelt was questioned by a friend about his use of water torture against detainees, he described it as 'an old Filipino method of mild torture.' 'Nobody,' he said, 'was seriously damaged.'[12]

The Bush administration largely avoided discussion of alleged use of torture in the United States in the aftermath of the September 11 attacks by use of subtle rhetoric. For example, in a speech delivered in September 2006, Bush said the following:

> We knew that [the al-Qaeda strategist] had more information that could save innocent lives, but he stopped talking. As his questioning proceeded, it became clear that he had received training on how to resist interrogation. And so the CIA used an alternative set of procedures. These procedures were designed to be safe, to comply with our laws, our Constitution, and our treaty obligations. The Department of Justice reviewed the authorized methods extensively and determined them to be lawful. I cannot describe the specific methods used – I think you

US TORTURE AFTER 9/11 (*cont.*)

understand why – if I did, it would help the terrorists learn how to resist questioning, and to keep information from us that we need to prevent new attacks on our country. But I can say the procedures were tough, and they were safe, and lawful, and necessary.[13]

To the Bush administration's credit, the alleged forms of torture tend to be relatively mild. The most commonly cited – waterboarding – is a form of water torture in which the victim is strapped face-up to a board and has his or her mouth and nose covered by a cloth, at which point water is poured over the victim's face. Algerian journalist Henri Alleg described waterboarding he experienced at the hands of French soldiers in 1957:

The rag was soaked rapidly. Water flowed everywhere: in my mouth, in my nose, all over my face ... I tried, by contracting my throat, to take in as little water as possible and to resist suffocation by keeping air in my lungs for as long as I could. But I couldn't hold on for more than a few moments. I had the impression of drowning, and a terrible agony, that of death itself, took possession of me ... In spite of myself, the fingers of both my hands shook uncontrollably. 'That's it! He's going to talk,' said a voice.[14]

The relative advantage of waterboarding is that, compared to other forms of water torture, it brings with it a low risk of drowning if carefully supervised – and it would be hard not to say that most other forms of torture are categorically worse. The relative disadvantage of waterboarding is that it is, without question, a form of water torture.

End of the line

The Eighth Amendment to the US Constitution prohibits cruel and unusual punishment, but 'cruel and unusual' is a relative term. In the US Crimes Act of 1790, for example, the same Congress that approved the Eighth Amendment apparently felt that execution followed by corpse mutilation was not a cruel or unusual punishment for treason. To this day, the issue of whether execution itself violates the Eighth Amendment remains controversial in the United States.

There are six types of execution still practiced in the industrialized world. All of them are problematic.

Lethal injection. The predominant form of execution in the United States, lethal injection involves the intravenous administration of three drugs designed to cause death quickly and with as little pain as possible.

- The first of the three drugs, sodium piothental, is supposed to render the execution painless by inducing a coma in the prisoner.
- The second drug, pancuronium bromide, causes muscle paralysis.
- The third drug, potassium chloride, stops the heart.

The problem arises when the sodium piothental is either administered incorrectly, or does not take effect. In such cases, a paralyzed prisoner can experience painful cardiac arrest – with no way to move, speak, or scream.

In December 2006, Angel Nieves Diaz was prepared for lethal injection in Florida. The execution took an astonishing thirty-four minutes. Medical examiners later determined that the needle used to inject the sodium piothental had penetrated his vein, injecting the drug into soft tissue deep in his arm. The injection itself would have been painful and, judging by the duration of the execution and visible signs that Diaz was in pain, the sodium piothental never entirely took effect. Following the Diaz execution, Florida and several other states declared a temporary moratorium on executions by lethal injection.

Gas chamber. Although large-scale Nazi use of the gas chamber during the Holocaust made it difficult to praise this execution method as humane, the administration of hydrogen cyanide was purported to be a painless form of capital punishment. Several lengthy, agonizing gas chamber executions suggested otherwise. In 1996, the ninth US Circuit Court of Appeals found that use of the gas chamber constituted cruel and unusual punishment. It is no longer in use in the United States.

Electric chair. Invented by Thomas Edison, the electric chair is a quintessentially American form of execution. It kills prisoners by sending 2,000 volts through their body, theoretically ending their lives instantly. In practice, faulty equipment and user error have led to horrific botched executions in which the prisoner was burned alive. The electric chair is not generally used, but some US states allow death row inmates to select it as an option.

Firing squad. A bullet through the heart courtesy of a firing squad may still be the most humane form of capital punishment, and it may be the most dignified – associated, as it is, with military executions. Several US states still allow death row inmates to choose the firing squad over other forms of death penalty.

Hanging. The traditional form of execution in the Western world, death by hanging is usually quick if it's done correctly. If the rope is not long enough, then slow death by strangulation may result. An excessively long rope can cause decapitation, but it is not clear whether that would be any more painful than a standard hanging from the point of view of the prisoner.

Beheading. The guillotine was a popular form of execution during the eighteenth and nineteenth centuries, though executioners in Saudi Arabia prefer a large, sturdy sword. Beheading is among the more gruesome types of execution, but it may also be among the most humane if performed in a single, quick stroke.

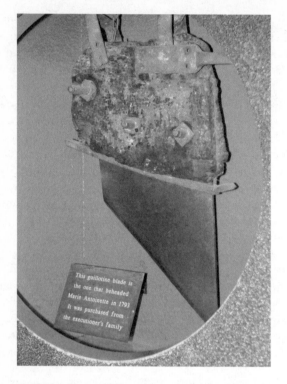

Figure 15 The guillotine blade used to execute Marie Antoinette, on display at Madame Tussaud's Museum, London.

6

Race and caste

The horror of class stratification, racism, and prejudice is that some people begin to believe that the security of their families and communities depends on the oppression of others, that for some to have good lives there must be others whose lives are truncated and brutal.

(Dorothy Allison, *Skin*)

We human beings aren't cannibals. We don't eat our own. We kill plants, we kill 'lower' animals, but we don't eat our own. So if there are human beings that those in power really want to exploit, whose lives and livelihoods they're prepared to sacrifice or have grown accustomed to sacrificing, then it's only natural to forget the humanity of the oppressed group. In the back of our minds, the oppressors make the oppressed – the others, whoever the others might be at the time – into strangers. That makes it easier to steal, to kill, to oppress. Just as we don't usually think about bleeding cows and orphaned calves and grinding slaughterhouses when we bite into a cheeseburger, we don't have to think about the effects our culture has on the people we've pushed outside of our field of vision.

This chapter discusses three types of discrimination – racism, class bias, and caste. These three types of discrimination ultimately operate in the same way, with the same effects, and usually for the same reasons. They are all insidious, they are all dangerous, and they are all so pervasive as to be unavoidable. The ancient disease we call bias seems to be both highly contagious and incurable. The best we can do is treat the symptoms.

Figure 16 The skulls of victims of the 1994 Rwandan genocide, which claimed over 800,000 lives.

Caste in India

India is as well known in the West for its caste system, perhaps, as it is for anything else. Unlike other countries that operate based on implicit castes, India's system is both ancient and explicated. While it lost official recognition with the Indian Constitution of 1950, it remains an unofficial reality of life.

There are approximately 165 million Dalits ('untouchables') in India who face racial profiling, segregation, discrimination, bonded labor, and violence. As Human Rights Watch reported in 1999:

> The offenses include forcing members of a scheduled caste or scheduled tribe to drink or eat any inedible or obnoxious substance; dumping excreta, waste matter, carcasses or any other obnoxious substance in their premises or neighborhood; forcibly removing their clothes and parading them naked or with painted face or body; interfering with their rights to land; compelling a member of a scheduled caste or scheduled tribe into forms of forced or bonded labor; corrupting or fouling the

water of any spring, reservoir or any other source ordinarily used by scheduled castes or scheduled tribes; denying right of passage to a place of public resort; and using a position of dominance to exploit a scheduled caste or scheduled tribe woman sexually.[1]

In March 2007, the UN Committee on the Elimination of Racial Discrimination identified 2005 data indicating that the number of reported hate crime incidents against Dalits has risen to more than 110,000 per year.[2] But because of police discrimination against Dalits, and the understandable reluctance of many Dalits to report hate crime incidents through official channels, this reflects only a tiny percentage of actual incidents. Indeed, police are often complicit in atrocities against Dalits. As Human Rights Watch reported in *Hidden Discrimination: Caste Violence Against India's 'Untouchables'*:

India's National Human Rights Commission (NHRC) – a statutory government body that the Indian government describes as the apex national institution to protect human rights and redress grievances – has commented that the law enforcement machinery is the greatest violator of Dalits' human rights. According to the NHRC, widespread custodial torture and killing of Dalits, rape and sexual assault of Dalit women, and looting of Dalit property by the police 'are condoned, or at best ignored' ...

Dalits are particularly vulnerable to arrest under draconian security laws. Additionally, under a theory of collective punishment, the police often target entire Dalit communities in search of one individual and subject them to violent search and seizure operations. Dalit women are particularly vulnerable to sexual violence by the police, which is used as a tool to punish Dalit communities. Police also allow private actors to commit violence against Dalits with impunity, and at times collude in committing such atrocities.[3]

High-profile incidents of abuse against Dalits illustrate a continuing social problem:

- On April 29, 2008, a young man noticed a six-year-old Dalit girl on his property in Uttar Pradesh, India. He responded by picking her up and throwing her into a pit of burning coals. The Indian government has charged him with attempted murder, and the case has galvanized Indian civil rights activists.[4]
- On May 30, 2008, a young Dalit man named Nirmal Singh was beaten to death by higher-caste youths in Chandigarh.[5]
- Thousands of Dalits converted to Christianity or Islam in hopes of escaping the caste hierarchy, which has been associated primarily with right-wing forms of Hinduism. In 2002, the government of Tamil Nadu attempted to restrict missionary activity by passing the Prohibition on Forcible Conversion of Religious Ordinance, which imposed criminal sanctions on any conversions deemed motivated by 'allurements or any fraudulent means.' The legislation was repealed later the same year.[6] Conversion has not, however, been as successful as one might hope as a means of escaping caste discrimination; in the Tamil Nadu village of Tirunelveli, over 1,000 recent Dalit converts to Christianity reconverted to Hinduism (with signed affidavits promising long-term allegiance) after two converts were lynched, and others violently assaulted, at the hands of upper-caste Christians.[7]

While the national government of India has spoken out strongly against racial discrimination, regional governments often ignore such claims and refuse to co-operate in enforcement of Indian human rights laws. But a combination of Dalit civil rights activism and increasing media coverage has brought more public attention to the issues that Dalits in India face.

Discrimination against Dalits is traditionally understood in terms of birth heritage, but in reality the Indian caste system has

Figure 17 Two low-caste girls in Phargang, a suburb of New Delhi, survive by collecting garbage. Although India does not enforce the traditional caste system as a point of policy, its effects continue.

color bias aspects to it as well – Dalits tend to have darker skin than members of other castes in a country where lighter skin tends to indicate higher social status. A recent advertisement for Fair and Lovely brand skin lightening cream, for example, features a dark-skinned upper-caste woman turned down for a job who returns home, applies the skin bleaching cream, and is accepted for employment after it takes effect. While not all Dalits are dark skinned, and not all dark-skinned Indians are Dalits, there is a strong correlation. (Other means of determining Dalit status tend to rely on existing income level, dialect, and family heritage.)

Discrimination against Dalits can also take a form similar to that of racial discrimination in other countries. In regions of the United States that operated under racial segregation policies, for example, black and white Americans were assigned different restrooms and drinking fountains; Dalits are expected to use separate wells in regions of India where caste status is strongly observed. In both cases, the assumption is that the higher caste, or the racial group that materially benefits from prejudice, would be rendered impure by integration.

Caste and whiteness

LEARNING TO DISCRIMINATE

Racism and classism are often treated as if they were complicated, mystical ideas beyond human understanding, but they're nearly always reducible to very simple motives. Here are a few of the more common motivations behind institutional prejudice:

International conflict. Two nations fail to get along, and many people in each nation begin to see people living in the other nation – and those who share their ethnic background – as the enemy. *Example:* The US internment of Japanese Americans during World War II.

Colonial presence. An indigenous culture is invaded by people belonging to a different ethnicity and a more technologically advanced culture, and the indigenous culture is exploited, relocated, or otherwise harmed for economic purposes. Over time, members of the colonial culture take efforts to defend its privileged status while members of the indigenous culture combat its injustice – and may learn to hate its perpetrators. *Example:* The situation faced by indigenous peoples in Africa, Australia, and the Americas following European colonization.

Immigration. A country with open or porous borders begins to experience an increase in immigration from a specific ethnic group. The immigrants, if not assimilated into the majority culture, can become targets of nativist prejudice and exploitation – especially if they are less affluent than the norm. *Example:* The situation faced by Moroccan immigrants in France, and by Mexican immigrants in the United States.

While the history of caste in India is unique, the experience of classism is universal. Even in Communist countries, where efforts are made to eliminate class distinctions, new ones emerge – stratified based on, if nothing else, perceived allegiance to the Party. North Korea, for example, enforces an explicit, strict three-tier caste system: wealthy families that are well regarded by local government officials are classified as high-caste or 'core' (*haeksim kyechung*), less wealthy families are classified as middle-caste or 'wavering' (*tongyo kyechung*), and families that are ostracized are classified as low-caste or 'hostile' (*joktae kyechung*).

In most other countries, caste distinctions are less explicit – but they are no less real, and there is no indication that they are diminishing. In the Western world, there is a very clear class stratification based on perceived wealth and land ownership. In the medieval era, there were the nobility, the tradesmen ('*bourgeoisie*'), and the peasants. Today we speak of a person, family, or neighborhood being upper-class, upper middle-class, middle-class, lower middle-class, working-class, or lower-class. While there is some level of class mobility, both wealth and poverty tend to be stable; people from wealthy families tend to stay wealthy, and people from poor families tend to stay poor. Class also tends to correlate with region and race or ethnic identity. Alaska, Mississippi, and eight other US states have no billionaires; California has ninety, New York forty-four.[8] African-Americans are three times as likely to live in poverty as white Americans. Downtown luxury lofts are often easy walking distance from housing projects and homeless shelters. The major cities of Brazil, such as Rio de Janeiro and San Paolo, are beautiful and attract a considerable number of wealthy tourists, from whom the underdeveloped city slums are well hidden.

In Western cultures, the primary cultural divide has been racial – between those deemed 'white' and those deemed 'non-white.' Racism in other nations can take other forms, as in the case of the anti-Tutsi Rwandan genocide of 1994 and the anti-Kurd Iraqi Anfal campaign of 1986–8, but in Britain, the United States, Canada, Europe, Australia, and parts of Asia, humans of

Figure 18 A homeless black man smokes in Rio de Janeiro, Brazil. Although overt racial discrimination has become socially unacceptable in most of the world, institutional racism remains a fact of life. The slave trade and the racial caste system used to support it has impoverished most majority-black nations, and led to disproportionate poverty among black residents of non majority-black nations.

white ancestry tend to be given more opportunities and higher social status than members of other ethnic backgrounds. This is because of a racial caste system centuries in the making.

In ancient times, however, race was defined in different terms. The Egyptian *Book of Gates* (*c.* fourteenth century BCE) organized humanity into four races: Asiatics, Egyptians, Libyans, and Nubians. None of these races were considered white, and there was no clear correlation between social status and skin color; the panel depicts Egyptians themselves as the second-darkest race. The Hebrew Bible passage granting extended blessings and curses to the descendants of the three sons of Noah – Ham, Shem, and Japheth – is generally read as a racial taxonomy, but it is not entirely clear which modern ethnic groups would fall under each designation. In any case, the passage extends the greatest blessings to the ostensibly Middle Eastern children of Shem, not the ostensibly European children of Japheth.

The origin of the white supremacist caste system can probably be traced to Greco-Roman culture, not because Greco-Roman law imposed it but because Greek and Roman rulers and aristocrats happened to be of predominantly European ancestry. Until Greece, there had been no dominant European empire of any kind – the seat of the Western world having been primarily in the Middle East and northern Africa. And even during the Greco-Roman era, there was no pan-European concept of whiteness; non-Greek Europeans were described by Aristotle as 'full of spirit, but wanting in intelligence and skill' and 'unable to rule over others,' attributes that he seemed to blame on the 'cold climate' of the region.[9] As the Roman Empire spread into Europe, however, it became increasingly identified with European culture. And as leaders hailing from indigenous European barbarian tribes began to gain power, European empires led by whites began to dominate the Western world.

At the same time that imperial power became associated with whites, the opposite end of the white supremacist caste system began to take shape as black slavery started to emerge. To a casual observer, Africa has a remarkable amount of indigenous ethnic diversity – second only to Asia. The median height of a Maasai man from modern-day Kenya, for example, is greater than six feet, among the world's tallest, while an average Aka man of central Africa stands at less than five feet, among the world's shortest. The height, build, facial features, languages, religion, recipes, fashion, government structure, and political allegiances of ancient Africa were diverse, and they remain diverse, but to the white Western eye the sprawling, mysterious continent and its people were slaves, black slaves, and little else.

The widespread export of black slaves began in the seventh century CE in the Middle East. By the time Portuguese trader Antão Gonçalves purchased the first African–European slave in 1441, the empires of the Western world had already had eight centuries to grow accustomed to the idea that dark, African skin most likely meant that the person had chattel status. Although most chattel slavery was abolished in the nineteenth century, overtly racist laws remained on the books in many purportedly advanced Western nations until the latter half of the twentieth.

MODERN-DAY SLAVERY

According to Anti-Slavery International, approximately twenty-seven million people are still enslaved worldwide. There are three primary types of slavery:

Chattel slavery. Slavery in which a person is bought and sold as property. This is the type that existed in the United States and much of Europe, and it still remains common in some remote areas of China (which did not officially end slavery until 1910), the Middle East, and sub-Saharan Africa.

Forced labor. Slavery that is conditional on the threat of violence or arrest.

Indentured servitude. Also known as bonded labor, this is forced labor used to pay a debt – often a debt that is too big ever to pay off, and/or carried on for multiple generations.

The American experiment

The racial caste hierarchy doesn't just affect Westerners of European and African ancestry. As European nations assumed colonial control over the Americas, Australia, Africa, and some parts of Asia, they displaced – and, more often than not, violently displaced – pre-existing indigenous societies. No act of colonial violence more starkly symbolizes this pattern than the near-extermination of the indigenous American-Indian population during the European settlement of the Americas. While it is not clear how many deaths were due to intentional execution and how many were the indirect results of disease, starvation due to displacement, and other factors, approximately ninety-five percent of the indigenous American population died as a result of colonialism.[10] As University of Hawaii professor David Stannard describes it:

> [T]he ratio of native survivorship in the Americas following European contact was less than half of what the human survivorship ratio would be in the United States today if every single white person and every single black person died ... [F]ar from the heroic and romantic heraldry that customarily is used to symbolize the European settlement of the Americas, the emblem most congruent with reality would be a pyramid of skulls.[11]

This adds a particular irony to the US illegal immigration debate. There are approximately twelve million Latinos living in the United States without immigration paperwork, and most of them are of Amerindian or *mestizo* (mixed Spanish and Amerindian) ancestry. According to a March 2007 poll, twenty-four percent of Americans support the forcible deportation of all undocumented immigrants – which remains the official policy of the US government.[12] More than four centuries after the first European colony was established in North America, the descendent of its colonial government is still in the business of forcibly displacing people of indigenous ancestry.

There is no ethnic group that has gone completely untouched by racism and racial caste systems. To be a Jew, for example, is to have in one's history the full saga of the Jewish diaspora, including the Holocaust and the two millennia of exclusion, violence, and threats of genocide that preceded it.

Even Anglo-Saxons, the ethnic group most commonly associated with the word 'white,' can look back on the oppression of indigenous English following the Norman conquest of 1066. But the point could be legitimately argued that the Amerindian ethnic group is the most oppressed in human history – the population of two continents subjugated, exploited, and nearly driven out of existence. To this day, descendants of indigenous Canadians are statistically more likely to commit suicide than members of any other identifiable ethnic group on Earth.

Paving the road to hell

The motivations behind American slavery were clear, but sometimes what might sound on the surface to be a benevolent approach towards race can be just as exploitative in its own way.

Beginning in 1869, but escalating with the Aborigines Protection Amending Act of 1915, the Australian government took native children from their parents and made them wards of the state. These children became known as the Stolen Generations. The policy was formally in effect until 1969, and lasted in practice for at least a decade beyond that.

The reasons behind the legalized kidnapping of these children often sounded reasonable on the surface. The children, it was argued, were at greater risk in the low-tech indigenous world where modern health care was not available; indigenous populations were dying off in some instances, and there might not be enough people to care for the children; and so forth.

A.O. Neville, who oversaw the relocation of countless indigenous children from 1915 to 1940, is an illustration of the harm that ostensibly well-intentioned people can do. While many white Australians were terrified of racial integration and mixed-race relationships, for example, Neville staunchly advocated both the biological and social integration of indigenous Australians into the more affluent white population, which he believed would end discrimination against indigenous Australians. He saw this as the only means to eliminate poverty and reduce the suffering of Australia's indigenous population:

> So few of our own people as a whole are aware of the position [of indigenous Australians]. Yet we have had the coloured man amongst us for a hundred years or more. He has died in his hundreds, nay thousands, in pain, misery, and squalor, and through avoidable ill-health. Innumerable little children have perished through neglect and ignorance. The position, in some vital respects, is not much better today [in 1948] than it was fifty years ago. Man is entitled to a measure of happiness in his life. Yet most of these people have never known real happiness. Some are never likely to know it. The causes of their condition are many. Mainly it is not their fault, it is ours, just as it lies with us to put the matter right.[13]

A person living in the American South in 1948 with these sorts of attitudes towards the effects of institutional white racism on non-white populations might have been a strong opponent of segregation, but in Australia Neville's role, and the role of ostensibly well-intentioned people, was decidedly destructive. According to Australia's Reconciliation Network, approximately ten percent of Australian aboriginal and Torres Strait islander children were abducted under Australia's assimilation policies. The kidnapping of children from their families was traumatic to begin with, and when they were placed in poorly managed, underfunded, racist institutions that offered them a far less pleasant environment than the indigenous communities from which they came, the end result was increased poverty and disease, coupled with immeasurable damage to indigenous communities. The policy also ended any prospect of positive relations between indigenous communities and the Australian government, and the effects of this policy on such relations still linger to this day.

But on paper, Neville's views sounded sensible relative to the views of most of his white contemporaries. This highlights the importance of looking for racism in the *effects* of a policy, and not necessarily just in the motives behind it. A.O. Neville was not a racist man by the standards of his time, but he administered some of the most profoundly racist policies in Australian history. His victims would have probably been better off if he were more of a snarling bigot, as bigotry could have dissuaded him from pursuing the disastrous sweeping social policy of forced assimilation.

The end of Western institutional racism?

Racism as we know it today in Britain and the United States is contingent on two factors: a racial caste system that benefits whites, and relative racial segregation. Both of these factors, for various reasons, have an expiration date. It is highly likely that by the end of the twenty-first century, the white racial caste system will have dissipated.

The Eurocentric Western racial caste system emerged when the people in power began to be identified as whites – in other words, when European empires of Greece and Rome began to supersede the north African and Middle Eastern empires of Egypt and Mesopotamia. This pattern has continued more or less unabated for over two millennia – initially due to the power of empires and their colonial reach, and more recently due to early industrialization of North America and Europe.

But the age of European colonial empires has long since ended, and Asia will soon surpass North America and Europe in industrialization and economic power. Economists predict that by 2050, the Chinese economy will achieve parity with the US economy.[14] India will soon follow. But even China and India will not hold the sort of monopoly over industrialization initially held by the United States and Europe. As economist Jeffrey Sachs notes:

> Countries throughout Asia are working hard to overcome past strategic animosities in order to create increasingly integrated flows of merchandise, finance, and technology. On the basis of current trends, and as a very rough estimate, this integrated Asian economy could reach about half of world GNP (up from a current one-third), with about 60% of the world's population.[15]

Economic growth in the Global South, while not yet comparable to pan-Asian economic growth, is also substantial. In Africa, per capita income climbed at a steady annual rate of 1.9 percent from 1995 to 2006.[16] Per capita income growth in Latin America trends higher, climbing to 3.8 percent for 2006.[17] While there is no reason to believe that the prosperity of the United States and Europe will not continue, their *relative* prosperity will decrease over time. The economic power of the world will become better distributed, the wielders of that power more ethnically diverse.

As of the 2001 census, the British population is ninety-one percent white. In 2051, if current projections hold, Britain will be seventy-one percent white.[18] The United States is also becoming more ethnically diverse. As of the 2000 Census, the US population was seventy-five percent white.[19] By 2050, if current projections hold, the United States will be fifty percent white.[20] In both countries, this can be attributed primarily to an increase in immigration and a decline in the white birth rate – non-white British women have an average of 2.2 children, for example, while white British woman have an average of 1.6 children.[21]

As the population becomes more diverse and interracial marriages more socially acceptable, the number of multiracial families will also increase. A 2005 Cornell University study found that sixteen percent of respondents aged 24–5 were in an interracial dating relationship at the time; among Latinos aged 24–5, the figure was thirty-three percent.[22] While it is too early to make solid predictions regarding the impact of interracial marriage on long-term population diversity, there will certainly be an impact.

Race and civil rights today

The message of economics and democracy is clear: Within the next half-century, predominantly white North America and Europe will wield less relative power in the global economy, even as both regions will begin to adopt a more multiracial identity. Whether white institutional racism dies during this century or staggers weakly into the next, it is living on borrowed time.

Unfortunately, borrowed time is all any of us have. Every day, institutional racism outlives a few thousand victims more. Even if Eurocentric institutional racism is on the way out, its impact on human life will be felt for generations to come. Here are a few examples of the ways in which institutional racism still poses a threat to civil liberties:

Racial profiling. This circumstance, in which many law enforcement officials treat people of color with undue suspicion or hostility, is common in the United States, Canada, and Britain. The most easily documented form of racial profiling is what civil rights activists refer to as the 'driving while black' phenomenon – the decision by law enforcement officers to stop and search vehicles specifically because they are driven by black or Latino motorists. A 2003 study conducted by the University of Minnesota Law School, for example, discovered that black motorists were three times as likely to be pulled over as whites, even though whites were twice as likely to have contraband in their vehicles.[23]

But racial profiling is not limited to drivers, as the story of Sharon Simmons-Thomas demonstrates. Simmons-Thomas was leaving a department store in the Bronx in December 2002 when she was reportedly detained on suspicion of shoplifting. Despite providing department store security with receipts documenting her purchases, she was reportedly handcuffed for three hours in a windowless room, insulted, threatened with violence, and eventually sent on her way – minus her purchases, for which she had already paid.[24]

The racially charged US immigration debate has also been linked to racial profiling. One case that made headlines in 2006 was that of thirty-seven-year-old Bettina Casares, a US citizen and Air Force veteran returning home after visiting her family in Mexico. After being stopped by Border Patrol, she was arrested, thrown across a room, beaten, threatened, and detained for several hours. It did not matter that she was a US citizen and military veteran; she was a woman of Mexican-American ancestry, and that was enough. After finally making it back to the United States, she photographed her injuries and successfully filed suit against the US government. She was awarded an undisclosed settlement.[25]

Job discrimination. While the US Civil Rights Act of 1964 technically bans workplace discrimination, it stands to reason that most employers don't announce their decisions to discriminate on the basis of race – and studies have confirmed that job discrimination remains a serious problem.

One study was particularly damning. In 2003, researchers at Northwestern University prepared a group of job applicants – all comparably well-qualified, some black, some white, some with criminal records, and some without – and sent them off to apply for jobs in Milwaukee, Wisconsin. The racial disparity was immediately apparent: thirty-four percent of the white applicants with no criminal record were called back for an interview, compared to fourteen percent of black applicants.

Worse: Seventeen percent of white applicants *with* a criminal record were called back for interviews. In other words, employers were more likely to choose a white candidate with a criminal record than they were to choose a black candidate without one.[26]

In France, discrimination between white and black job applicants is even more stark. One 2005 study found that while the nation's overall unemployment rate for university graduates was five percent, the unemployment rate for university graduates of North African origin was 26.5 percent – more than five times as high.[27]

Housing discrimination. While the US Civil Rights Act of 1964 bans employment discrimination, the Civil Rights Act of 1968 bans housing discrimination. Unfortunately, it is equally easy to circumvent.

Researchers were able to document this particularly well in the aftermath of Hurricane Katrina. Multiple studies showed a

Figure 19 A home in New Orleans' Lower 9th Ward, destroyed by Hurricane Katrina in August 2005. The predominantly African-American 9th Ward, in which sixty percent of residents owned their own homes, was disproportionately affected by the storm. A combination of storm damage, federal and city policy, and housing discrimination has drastically reduced the African-American population of the city on a long-term basis.

pattern of racial discrimination by landlords; one of the strongest was conducted in 2006 by the National Fair Housing Alliance and Stanford University linguist John Baugh. Baugh set up audio recorders and enlisted a team of black and white volunteers to call local landlords, describing themselves as Katrina victims, and ask about pricing terms. In sixty-six percent of cases, white callers received more favorable terms. This example illustrates the pattern:

> In Birmingham, a White tester was told that she would not need to pay a security deposit or application fee, on account of her status as a Katrina survivor. She was also told she needed to make 2.5 times the rent to qualify for the apartment. The African-American tester was told that she would have to pay $150 for the security deposit and a $25 application fee for each applicant. The African-American hurricane survivor was also told that she would have to make three times the rent to qualify for the apartment.[28]

Job and housing discrimination are just two of the many ways to limit the social mobility of low-income people of color that are used throughout the Western world. More vigilant enforcement of civil rights laws could prevent particularly egregious examples of this phenomenon, but the overall pattern is much too subtle, and has become much too normal, to be completely addressed by anything other than a radical reorientation in the way that Western cultures view race and civil rights.

7

Gender and sexuality

There is more difference within the sexes than between them.

(Ivy Compton-Burnett, *Mother and Son*)

The biological sexes are real, but gender is a social construct. Pre-industrial societies created rote gender roles that played to each sex's relative strengths. To men, who tended to have more muscle mass with which to spear game, was relegated the role of provider. To women, who alone could bear and nurse children, was relegated the role of caregiver and forager. These mandatory gender roles no longer serve a practical purpose in most cultures today, but over the millennia they have marbled with nearly every religious, moral, and legal tradition to the point where they have become sacred. And because these gender roles are sacred, they result in both institutional sexism and the child of institutional sexism that we call heteronormativity.

Gender feels fundamental to human culture because it is. Over a period of centuries, ethnic and nationalistic distinctions change; wars are forgotten, civilizations collapse, families inter-marry. If history tells us anything, it is that time will ultimately kill nearly all of the human prejudices we live with today and replace them with innovative new ones. But sexism is different. Sexism is immortal, as old as the oldest records of human civilization. This is why, while it would probably be a mistake to say that sexism is *worse* than other forms of oppression (as if oppression were quantifiable), it would be no mistake to say that it is more fundamental. We know that specific forms of racism have died before, for example, so we know that they can, but the same cannot be said of any form of sexism – though its effects on the choices that women and men make is not as profound in most of the world as it has been in the past.

Violence and power

While the two traditional gender roles are complementary, they are not, in most cultures, equal. Women have made considerable gains in recent decades, but men still tend to reign supreme over tribes, armies, corporations, churches, universities, and nations while women are relegated to the background. Why is this?

Perhaps it has something to do with the cause-and-effect relationship between power and violence. It is no coincidence that the oldest heroes of the Western tradition are for the most part not great thinkers or great nurturers, but rather great conquerors. We look back in our religious and folkloric traditions upon Gilgamesh, slayer of the Heavenly Bull; David, slayer of Goliath; Kintu, slayer of Bemba; Perseus, slayer of the Gorgons; Hercules, slayer of the seven-headed hydra; Rama, slayer of the demon Ravana; Susanoo, slayer of the dragon Orochi. Even Jesus Christ, a rare exception to the myth of the violent hero, is expected to return, cast Satan into a pit of fire, and reconquer the armageddon-torn world so that he may reign over it as king.

The two essential roles we tend to associate with power are those of protector and conqueror. Powerful people help us keep what we have and take what we need. Because men tend to have higher muscle mass and a subsequently higher capacity for physical violence, old civilizations and old institutions portrayed them as better protectors and better conquerors – and today, despite the fact that inflicting physical violence on others is not generally part of day-to-day life, the old image of the male protector-conqueror sticks. This image is reinforced by the image of the male hunter, the male soldier, the male police officer, the male boxer, the male action film star, and so forth. Men protect, conquer, and provide. That is their function in the traditional gender role system. Their greater aggregate brute strength and associated capacity for violence has bought them at least 6,000 years of social dominance.

This dominance has, of course, been profoundly unjust. But it has also handicapped the human race. In the industrialized world, cultures that practice institutional sexism – which is to say, all cultures to a greater or lesser degree – create practical problems for themselves. Sexism reduces specialized talent pools. If women cannot lead nations, then the talent pool of potential national leaders is reduced in size by fifty-one percent. If women cannot lead corporations, then the talent pool of potential corporate administrators is reduced in size by fifty-one percent. If women cannot succeed as engineers, then the talent pool of potential engineers is reduced in size by fifty-one percent. When we consider the number of medical and technological achieve-ments that still elude us, as a species, the costs of institutional sexism become especially profound. What if the person who *would* have developed a cure for cancer fifty years ago was excluded from medical school, and pushed into a traditional housewife role? What if the person who *would* have invented a clean, abundant, renewable energy source thirty years ago was laughed out of Physics 101? Because it prevents a majority of human beings from participating in important large-scale decisionmaking processes, institutional sexism lobotomizes our culture – effectively reducing the collective IQ of the human species by half.

Then there is the effect these gender roles have on men. Men are taught to be violent, dominant, and competitive, to master and subjugate the world around them, to hide their emotions and their capacity to nurture. They are taught, in effect, to be conquerors and subjugators. So it should come as no surprise that so many men who are frustrated with life and find the masculine ideal impossible to achieve turn to crime – with tragic consequences.

Women's response

In a Western context, feminism tends to be categorized into three 'waves:'

- **First-wave feminism**. This focused exclusively on securing basic legal rights for women – the right to vote, for example, or to own property. Historically, the first wave is generally regarded as having lasted from 1792, the publication year of Mary Wollstonecraft's *A Vindication of the Rights of Woman*, until World War II.
- **Second-wave feminism**. This focused on securing rights and equal protection for women consistent with their emerging roles in the workforce and the political sphere. The second wave is generally regarded as having begun during World War II, when women started taking on traditionally 'male' jobs to replace men sent off to war.
- **Third-wave feminism**. A term coined by Rebecca Walker in 1992, describing an emerging feminism that addresses both the concerns of women and intersectional concerns – issues disproportionately faced by women of color, by lesbian, bisexual, and transgender women, and by other women whose lives were not adequately addressed by the predominantly white, heterosexual women who led the second-wave feminist movement.

But this categorization is somewhat misleading, because the differences among the waves are more generational than philosophical. Someone who was primarily active as a feminist during the 1970s,

WHAT IS INTERSECTIONALITY?

Critical race theorist Kimberle Crenshaw coined the term 'intersectionality' while she was a student at Harvard Law School during the early 1980s. In a March 2004 interview, she explained the reasoning behind the term:

> [The concept of intersectionality] grew out of trying to conceptualize the way the law responded to issues where both race and gender discrimination were involved. What happened was like an accident, a collision. Intersectionality simply came from the idea that if you're standing in the path of multiple forms of exclusion, you are likely to get hit by both. These women are injured, but when the race ambulance and the gender ambulance arrive at the scene, they see these women of color lying in the intersection and they say, 'Well, we can't figure out if this was just race or just sex discrimination. And unless they can show us which one it was, we can't help them.'[1]

Perhaps no ruling better signifies the concept of intersectionality than the US eighth Circuit Court of Appeals' ruling in *DeGraffenreid v. General Motors Assembly Division* (1977), in which five black women sued for discrimination on the basis of both race and gender: '[T]his lawsuit must be examined to see if it states a cause of action for race discrimination, sex discrimination, or alternatively either, but not a combination of both.'

But women of color do, in fact, face both race and sex discrimination – and there is no way to extricate one from the other. To the extent that the legal framework and our culture at large tell people who face discrimination on multiple grounds that they must choose one identity and stick to it – that women of color can be thought of as implicitly white women or as implicitly male people of color, but may not be treated as women of color – it ignores intersectional concerns.

This is unfortunate for many reasons, one being that people who face multiple categories of discrimination also tend to face the most severe forms of discrimination. Someone who harbors

> ## WHAT IS INTERSECTIONALITY? (*cont.*)
>
> prejudices against women and people of color might be inclined to hire someone who fits in one category, but not necessarily someone who fits in both.
>
> In recent years, the term 'intersectionality' has broadened to refer to any situation in which a person faces discrimination on multiple grounds.

for example, would probably qualify as a second- rather than third-wave feminist, even if she held third-wave ideals.

The language of feminist waves has more to do with how feminism's priorities have changed over time than it does with individual beliefs, which are more complicated. Individual feminist beliefs, instead, tend to be classified into one or more of these three movements:

- **Liberal feminism**. This emphasizes policy reform as the primary vehicle for the advancement and preservation of gender equality. Liberal feminists tend to focus less on changing the culture or promoting gender solidarity, and more on changing policies that have an oppressive effect on women.
- **Radical feminism**. This welcomes policy reform but also seeks an end to gender roles as they are currently understood. Radical feminists tend to question the idea of gender, and focus on challenging institutional sexism by promoting a more flexible view of gender. In the short term, radical feminism also tends to be supportive of gender solidarity – giving support to groups and institutions made up of women, whose voices are not adequately heard in the political mainstream.
- **Cultural feminism**. This tends to shy away from policy reform and focus more on building independent social

power structures operated by women based on traditional feminine principles. While radical feminists view gender itself as a problematic concept, cultural feminists tend to embrace it as reflective of deep and insurmountable differences between the sexes.

Regardless of how one might self-identify, no person of conscience can legitimately dispute that institutional sexism is a very real problem with very real consequences.

Violence against women

Today, the consequences of institutional sexism are still being felt. There is no clearer indication of this than government responses to sexual violence:

- United States: A sixteen-year-old girl is drugged unconscious and then brutally gang-raped by a group of three young men, one of whom is the son of the local assistant sheriff. The men capture the twenty-one-minute rape on video, removing all doubt that they had committed the act, so the defense attorney argues that the girl, whom he described as a 'slut,' had consented in advance to being drugged unconscious and repeatedly raped. Astonishingly, the strategy actually paid off when the first jury deadlocked in June 2004. The rapists were convicted in a March 2006 retrial and each were sentenced to six-year prison sentences, with possibility of early release in less than three years.[2]
- Saudi Arabia: A woman is gang-raped fourteen times by a group of men. In November 2007, the Saudi government sentences her to 200 lashes and six months in prison for violating sex-segregation laws.[3]
- Uganda: A five-year-old girl living in the Amuru district is raped by a twenty-seven-year-old man. The case against her perpetrator is strong and includes biological evidence, severe

physical trauma to the girl, and the testimony of two witnesses – one who could vouch that she had been taken to her assailant's home, another who interrupted the rape in progress. But police officers refused to investigate because the girl's father was unable to pay the officers' 'investigation fee,' or bribe, of 60,000 Ugandan shillings.[4]

Both rape and domestic violence tend to go underreported and, when reported, underprosecuted. In Britain, for example, one in twenty women are victims of rape, only one out of four victims report rape, and only 5.7 percent of women reporting rape see their attackers convicted. Subsequently, over 99.9 percent of British rapes go unpunished.[5] In the United States, the Commonwealth Fund has estimated that approximately three million women are victims of domestic violence each year;[6] fewer than one-third of these cases are reported.[7]

Addressing violence against women can be made difficult by many factors. Among them:

- Most instances of violence against women take place in private; domestic violence is generally committed by intimate partners or members of the family, and about sixty percent of rapes take place in the victim's home or the home of a friend or family member.[8] This reduces the chances that the crime will be witnessed.
- Most victims – sixty-two percent of rape victims, for example[9] – know their attacker. They might feel guilty about reporting someone they know to the police, or might fear retaliation.
- There is still considerable victim-shaming and social stigma attached to violence against women, particularly rape. Even after rape is reported, there can be a presumption of consent by people who know both the victim and the assailant.

There are various approaches to these issues, some more controversial than others. When there are no witnesses to the crime of rape, medical examination of the victim can provide physical evidence that a rape has taken place, and can even provide irrefutable evidence of the attacker's identity. Public education initiatives can reduce the stigma associated with rape and domestic assault, and make it less difficult for victims to come forward. Vigilant enforcement of protection orders, and increased funding for battered women's shelters, can provide greater security for victims.

WHY IS VIOLENCE AGAINST WOMEN A CIVIL LIBERTIES ISSUE?

The ACLU Women's Rights Project addresses issues pertaining to violence against women. Some of you may be asking yourselves why. After all, isn't violence against women sort of like violence against men?

It's exactly like violence against men – but it isn't addressed in the same way. Men who are victims of violence have historically received greater protection from the criminal justice system than women who are victims of violence. They are more likely to be victimized in front of witnesses; they tend to be closer in physical size to their assailants, which in many cases makes them better able to retaliate; they are more likely to be taken seriously by law enforcement officials.

Rape and domestic violence are also tools of power, of dominance. They contribute to gender inequality. Rape is a weapon of war in military conflict, and always has been – in ancient Rome, men and women alike were raped by soldiers as a means of demonstrating dominance.

The essential purpose of government is to prevent citizens from committing violence against each other. To the extent that men can commit violence against women with impunity, violence against women speaks to – and contributes to – the equal protection differential between women and men. It represents the failure of government to provide equal protection to all citizens, regardless of gender.

But what is also needed is greater attention by prosecutors to include marginalized women who do not have access to information, services, and social contacts available to middle-class women. An American woman is three times as likely to report rape, for example, if she is white rather than black.[10] And studies have consistently found that between seventy-five and ninety percent of American Indian women in chemical addiction treatment programs are victims of rape.[11] The government has an obligation to provide all women with the tools and information they need to protect themselves and prevent their assailants from harming others.

Gender apartheid

Sex segregation remains a part of Western culture and institutional life. In some contexts, it is generally seen as practical and harmless – segregated restrooms, for example, being the norm in many countries. But there are other instances in which gender segregation can have a more profound effect on the rights of women.

In 2007, it would have been unthinkable openly to create public schools with the specific, deliberate, and public goal of racial segregation. But the public school gender segregation movement is moving ahead in the United States, and shows no signs of slowing.

Equal educational opportunity in the United States is protected by Title IX of the Patsy T. Mink Equal Opportunity in Education Act, which reads: 'No person in the United States shall, on the basis of sex, be excluded from participation in, be denied the benefits of, or be subjected to discrimination under any education program or activity receiving Federal financial assistance.'[12]

In 2004, the US Department of Education proposed new

Figure 20 In this 1917 public school home economics class, girls are taught how to cook meals in preparation for lives as full-time homemakers.

regulations to permit the establishment of single-sex schools and single-sex classes. This sounds innocent enough at first, but the new regulations themselves suggest a scenario that could become problematic:

> If the results of the survey [of parents] show a strong preference for a single-sex class in chemistry for girls, while for boys there is no expressed interest in any single-sex classes, the school in this example would not violate these proposed provisions by creating a single-sex chemistry class for girls without creating a single-sex class for boys. However, the school would be required [if there is no single-sex class for boys] to provide a substantially equal coeducational chemistry class.[13]

Because the classes in question need not be similar, only 'substantially equal,' the following immediately come to mind as possibilities:

- A girls-only home economics class is established where the teacher reinforces traditional gender roles by attempting to persuade girls to become full-time homemakers. In the background is the extremely unpopular coeducational home economics class, where a bored teacher and an even more bored group of predominantly male students show up for extra credit.

- Segregated character education classes are established to instill traditional gender roles in boys and girls. Students are graded based on their ability to conform to gender norms.
- A boys–only physics class is established and taught by a dynamic instructor who happens to believe that girls aren't very good at science. The coeducational physics class is taught by the gym teacher.

These scenarios may sound far-fetched, but they – or ones very much like them – would be the inevitable result of gender-segregated school programs designed by conservative local school boards. If the programs are segregated, then the objective of 'substantially equal' educational experiences cannot be achieved. As Chief Justice Earl Warren wrote in *Brown v. Board of Education* (1954):

> We conclude that, in the field of public education, the doctrine of 'separate but equal' has no place. Separate educational facilities are inherently unequal. Therefore, we hold that the plaintiffs and others similarly situated for whom the actions have been brought are, by reason of the segregation complained of, deprived of the equal protection of the laws guaranteed by the Fourteenth Amendment.

And even if the foundational argument of *Brown v. Board of Education* were unsound – even if it were somehow possible to have a segregated school system that manages to provide students with an equal educational experience – the public school system, by training children to socialize only with members of the same sex, would be laying the groundwork for the students to practice increased self-segregation as adults.

In her 1977 classic *Men and Women of the Corporation*, Harvard business professor Rosabeth Moss Kanter coined the term 'homosocial reproduction' to describe the tendency of executives to promote people who are most like themselves. Whites tend to promote whites; blacks tend to promote blacks; Latinos tend to promote Latinos; and, most significantly for this chapter, men tend to promote men. People grow accustomed to socializing with those who share their life experiences and so, to maximize their own comfort, they subconsciously tend to surround themselves with such people. Fortunately, it's not difficult for a well-meaning person to realize that he or she is doing this and make a sincere effort to stop. Unfortunately, it's clear that not that many people in the upper echelons of business and politics have made the attempt.

When *Fortune* magazine released its 2007 list of the 500 largest American public corporations based on gross revenue, 487 of the corporations had male CEOs.[14] This is a significant improvement over fifteen years ago, when 498 of the corporations had male CEOs, but it still represents a gender disparity that can't be explained by lifestyle trends alone. This gender disparity is also represented in politics; 19.5 percent of MPs in the British House of Commons are women,[15] compared to 16.5 percent of women in the US Congress.[16] While candidacies are often thought of as bottom-up, grassroots attempts by individual candidates to run for office, key donors and well-connected party officials tend to determine which candidacies are viable and which are not. In this respect, the relative dearth of women in public office also reflects homosocial promotion.

Civil rights laws can prevent overt discrimination, but because homosocial promotion is not an overt phenomenon it is not a situation that can be easily resolved from a public policy perspective. In Norway, Parliament introduced an innovative new strategy to increase the number of women in positions of corporate power: It mandated minimum quotas. Under the new

THE AMAZON LEGEND

While there have been societies in which women and men appeared to enjoy equal social status, and there have been women who ruled over large nations, there is not yet any evidence of an ancient culture whose institutions were ruled by women. The legend of the Amazons, a nation of warrior-women, appears to have little basis in history.

Homer's *Iliad* (most likely written during the seventh century BCE) contains two references to the ancient Amazons, 'those women as good as men' who were slain by the ancient hero Bellerophon.[18] Centuries later, the great Greek historian Herodotus (c. 484–25 BCE) would cite the Amazons in explaining the origins of the Scythians and Sarmatians, whose gender role dynamics baffled the ancient Greeks:

> [T]he Amazons used to scatter and go off some little distance in ones and twos to ease themselves, and the Scythians, when they noticed this, followed suit; until one of them, coming upon an Amazon girl all by herself, began to make advances to her. She did not resist and let him have her ...
>
> Having learnt of their success, the rest of the young Scythians soon succeeded in getting the Amazons to submit to their wishes. The two camps were then united ... Ever since then the women of the Sauromatae have kept to their old ways, riding to the hunt on horseback sometimes with, sometimes without, their men, taking part in war and wearing the same sort of clothes as men.[19]

Archaeological evidence of male and female warriors buried together has indicated that the Scythian and Sarmatian egalitarianism was very real, but the theory that this egalitarianism came about because of Scythian-Amazon intermarriage is much harder to substantiate. Given the wildly different account of the Amazons' fate given by Homer, it seems likely that the Amazons – if they existed at all – were not the nation of warrior-women that ancient writers portrayed them to be.

rules, which became mandatory in January 2008, public corporations must have a board of trustees that is at least forty percent female and forty percent male.[17]

Reproductive choice

If embryos and fetuses grew in petri dishes instead of women's bodies, then almost everyone would more than likely describe themselves as pro-life. But they grow in women's bodies, they are indeed parts of women's bodies, and this changes everything.

Civil liberties organizations tend to take pro-choice positions that are identified by the public, and sometimes by people within the respective organizations, as being focused primarily on the right to terminate a pregnancy. But this is only part of the full spectrum of a woman's reproductive choices – and none of these choices are made easy by a culture that dictates, and then condemns, every reproductive decision that women make.

Abstinence. The most fundamental reproductive right is the right not to have sex at all. This would seem to be the least controversial reproductive choice, but in some respects it is the most controversial. Consider:

- Sexual assault deprives women of their choice to refuse a sexual encounter. This is true not only of women who are violently raped, but also of women who are intoxicated to the point where they are no longer fully in control of their faculties. In 2005, a national poll of teenage girls discovered that twenty-six percent of Scottish fourteen-year-olds had had sex and that, of that twenty-six percent, sixty percent lost their virginity while drunk.[20] A similar 1997 US survey of teenage girls found that eighty-five percent 'identified drinking as a major factor leading to sex.'[21] Although sometimes characterized as 'gray rape,'[22] any instance in which women have sex without consent constitutes rape.

- Women are often pressured into having sex by their intimate partners. In a 1997 survey of US teenage girls, eighty-three percent cited pressure from her boyfriend as a crucial factor in the decision to have sex.[23]
- The social pressure to have sex is considerable, and the decision to abstain from sex is often seen as abnormal or otherwise socially unacceptable. In another recent survey of teenage girls, eighty-one percent who had sex indicated that they wished they had waited.[24]

The right to contraception, including emergency contraception. Governments have historically attempted to restrict women's access to birth control as a means of discouraging women from having sex, but this functions only to make women more vulnerable to unplanned pregnancy and sexually transmitted diseases.

The right to abortion. Governments have historically attempted to restrict women's access to abortion for two reasons – one noble but flawed, the other repressive. The noble motive is to protect the lives of embryos and fetuses. The less than noble motive is to restrict both birth control and abortion as a means of discouraging sexual activity.

Neither approach seems to be well served by abortion bans. This was well documented in a 2007 study by the World Health Organization, which determined that the legal status of abortion in a given country has no noticeable effect on its abortion rate.[25] Abortion is illegal in most of Latin America, for example, but over four million Latin American women have abortions each year anyway by taking easily obtained black market abortifacients – and, because they do so without medical supervision, their risk of permanent injury or death is far greater than it would be if they had undergone medically supervised abortions.[26]

Since abortion bans are ineffective at eliminating abortion, a more effective approach might be to look at the reasons why

Figure 21 Scene from the 2004 March for Women's Lives in Washington, DC. With 1.2 million participants, the pro-choice rally was the largest Capitol rally in US history.

women choose to have them. One 2005 US study described four common causes:

> Three-fourths of women cite concern for or responsibility to other individuals; three-fourths say they cannot afford a child; three-fourths say that having a baby would interfere with work, school or the ability to care for dependents; and half say they do not want to be a single parent or are having problems with their husband or partner.[27]

All of these causes would still apply regardless of the legality of abortion, but it seems likely that the work of private charities and public health initiatives already keeps the abortion rate lower than it would otherwise be, and that further investment in these areas could persuade more women not to have abortions.

The right to carry a pregnancy to term. Many women choose to become pregnant, or find themselves pregnant and decide to carry their pregnancy to term. The right to do so is not always protected. In China, for example, regional officials still mandate forced abortions in some cases – sometimes days before delivery, as occurred in the case of nineteen-year-old He Caigan:

> Family planning officials turned up at her house, in the countryside several hours outside Baise, before dawn on April 17 to force her to go to the hospital. This would have been her first baby – but she hadn't married the father, in contravention of family planning laws. She was already 9 months pregnant, just days away from delivery.
>
> 'They told me I'm too young, I couldn't keep the child and I should have an abortion,' she said. 'I'm too young to get a marriage certificate – I'm only 19 and my boyfriend's only 21.'[28]

As noted above, poverty and lack of child care also force many women who would not otherwise choose to have an abortion to terminate their pregnancies. Women are frequently denied the right to choose – the right to choose not to have sex, the right to choose safe sex, the right to terminate their pregnancies, and the right to continue their pregnancies. (Meanwhile, progressive governments hold that such decisions fall within what is often referred to in court decisions as a woman's 'zone of privacy.') Abortion is the most controversial part of the reproductive rights spectrum, but it does not by any means represent the only area in which women's reproductive rights are violated.

Lesbian, gay, bisexual, and transgender rights

There is nothing new about homosexuality. The oldest legal codes of Babylon, Egypt, and Sumer do not include prohibitions on gay sex between consenting, non-related people. Homosexuality was also common, and generally seen as socially acceptable, in ancient Greece and Rome. It occurs in nature. Issues of sexual orientation per se aside, the bodies of men and women are too similar for the idea of same-sex intercourse to be all that new or radical.

But when gender roles are mandated by law and procreation valued above all else, homosexuality tends to be prohibited. And those who crafted the old laws against homosexuality – Zoroastrian and Hebrew, for starters – must have found it to be a terrible temptation, since they apparently felt that nothing short of the death penalty would function as a suitable deterrent for male-on-male sexual intercourse. When lesbianism was a crime – in Puritan Massachusetts, for example – it was uniformly punished less severely than male homosexuality. If two men had sex, they could be hanged for it; if two women had sex, the punishment was a comparably mild flogging.

The histories of the United States and Britain with respect to sodomy laws are markedly different. By 1982, the British Isles had legalized same-sex intercourse – as early as 1967 in England and Wales. But in most of the United States, same-sex intercourse technically remained illegal – though the laws against it were seldom enforced – until 2003.

Today, decriminalization is not as much of an issue in the Western world as it once was. Gay sex is legal in Europe, Canada, the United States, and Mexico. But homosexuality remains criminalized in much of Asia and the Global South. In Africa, for example, homosexuality carries the death penalty in Mauritania and in Sharia-controlled regions of Nigeria, Somalia, and the Sudan; and in the Middle East, it is also punishable by death in Iran, Saudi Arabia, the United Arab Emirates, and Yemen.

In countries where living as a same-sex couple isn't illegal, there has been considerable interest in changing the law so that both opposite-sex and same-sex couples may participate in the

HOMOPHOBIA VS HETEROSEXISM

In 1967, psychiatrist George Weinberg coined the term 'homophobia' to refer to an irrational fear of, and/or hostility towards, lesbian and gay persons. Many psychologists regard homophobia as internal in origin – as a way of compensating for unwanted feelings of sexual attraction towards members of the same sex. Homophobia then becomes a way of reasserting one's heterosexuality, to oneself and to others, without having directly to confront personal questions of sexual identity. Gay and lesbian persons become a proxy, a way of expressing one's disapproval of one's own internal feelings of same-sex attraction without actually acknowledging that those feelings exist.

But homophobia is about psychology, not policy. Sodomy laws, for example, are not themselves homophobic because sodomy laws are not conscious entities and do not have phobias. Furthermore, even anti-gay policymakers can be motivated by factors other than homophobia – such as a desire to pander to homophobic constituents. Someone can oppose same-sex relationships based entirely on his or her own religious convictions, without any particular experience of homophobia. And some homophobes manage to act in a supportive way towards lesbians and gay men, just as others might overcome their personal phobias and private prejudices.

So clearly there is a distinction between the psychiatric phenomenon of irrational fear or hostility towards lesbians and gay men and policies or attitudes that have the effect of actually discriminating against, or otherwise harming, lesbians and gay men. Homophobia refers to the former. The term 'heterosexism,' referring to the latter, was coined by psychiatrist Stephen Morin during the late 1970s.

rights and responsibilities that come with marriage. There has been progress in this direction, although it has been slow.

Same-sex couples may legally marry in Belgium, Canada, the Netherlands, South Africa, Spain, and the US state of

Figure 22 Anti-gay protesters assemble outside of San Francisco City Hall to protest against same-sex marriage rights. Homophobia is one of the few forms of oppressive bigotry based upon identifiable groups that is still socially acceptable in industrialized nations, though this is beginning to change.

Massachusetts. Civil unions, granting some but not all of the rights that go along with marriage, are available in fourteen other countries, ten US states, and various major cities worldwide.

WHEN GENDER BECOMES A PRISON

According to contemporary gender theorists, there are two types of people: *cisgender* people, who more or less identify with their assigned gender role, and *transgender* people, who do not. For people who fall into the latter category, life can be challenging depending on the degree of transgender identity and the social circumstances of the person.

Many people could be described as at least very mildly transgender. I, for example, do not enjoy beer, sports, or most action films, and most of my friends are women. Men who live fully into their assigned gender role do not tend to identify as well with me as they do with most other men. To this extent, I am mildly *androgynous* – that is, less cisgender than the norm. A woman who does enjoy beer, sports, and action films, and who socializes primarily with men, would also be classified as mildly androgynous. People who are mildly androgynous can in fact experience discrimination grounded in the idea that they *should* have a stronger cisgender identity than they do. If my employer refuses to promote me because he can't trust a man who isn't macho, then that is a form of gender identity discrimination.

But mild androgyny is only the tip of the iceberg. Suppose my androgynous identity was *so* strong that I found the very idea of dressing, socializing, and otherwise identifying as a man to be inauthentic. Suppose I described myself using gender-neutral pronouns. Wouldn't I encounter a much stronger level of gender identity discrimination?

Let's carry this even further. Let's suppose that instead of being androgynous, for example simply *not* identifying in an authentic way with my assigned gender, I identified very strongly as a woman. Let's suppose that dressing as a woman, adopting a female name, and using feminine personal pronouns to describe myself was the only authentic way I could live. People who live in this way, who identify strongly as a member of a gender other than their assigned one, are referred to as *transsexual* – and they arguably encounter the most severe forms of gender identity discrimination.

WHEN GENDER BECOMES A PRISON (*cont.*)

If – as we discussed earlier in the chapter – gender roles are a social construct, then it stands to reason that this social construct will fit some people better than others. The idea that people who reject the gender role that is imposed upon them deserve the right to live an authentic and equal life is a relatively controversial idea, but it is an idea supported by every meaningful tradition of personal liberty. The most fundamental freedom is the freedom to be who we are, as long as no others are harmed in the process.

In 2003, Britain passed a law prohibiting discrimination on the basis of sexual orientation in the workplace. In thirty-eight US states, however, it remains perfectly legal to fire a lesbian, gay, bisexual, or transgender employee solely on the basis of sexual orientation or perceived gender identity. Some members of Congress have attempted to address this problem legislatively by adding sexual orientation and perceived gender identity to the list of protected categories defined in the Civil Rights Act of 1964. This effort has heretofore been unsuccessful, primarily due to right-wing opposition to the proposal.

8

The rights of the disabled

Disability is not a brave struggle or 'courage in the face of adversity.' Disability is an art. It is an ingenious way to live.

(Neil Marcus, quoted in Adam Benjamin,
*Making an Entrance: Theory and Practice for Disabled and
Non-Disabled Dancers*)

In 449 BCE, the Twelve Tables of Roman Law stipulated: '*Cito necatus insignis ad deformitatem puer esto*' ('a visibly deformed child must be put to death'). This sentence was generally carried out by throwing the child off a cliff. The language is very clear: It is 'must,' not 'may.' And 'deformed' refers not only to life-threatening disabilities, but to all visible disabilities. To be born with fused digits, for example, would have been a death sentence. To be born with a non-functioning arm or leg would have been a death sentence. There was no room, under Roman law, for those born with visible, manifest disabilities. And this legal standard, though not universally held, was by no means unique in the ancient world.

It is also, sadly, occasionally represented in the modern world as well. Slightly less than two millennia later, the Third Reich ruled over Germany. Its Nazi ideology of a perfect, economically powerful nation left no room for the disabled. Declared to be '*lebensunwertes Leben*' ('life unworthy of life'), some 200,000 people were killed under Germany's T-4 'Euthanasia' Program.

Figure 23 A plaque in memory of the approximately 275,000 disabled people executed by the Nazi regime under the T-4 Euthanasia Program.

Today, North Korea continues the practice of killing infants who are deemed unsuitable for life.

Discrimination against people with disabilities is one of the most ancient forms. We can reasonably assume that it's older than racism, older than class discrimination, older than homophobia. It is taken less seriously than it should be – people who would never dream of telling a racist, sexist, or homophobic joke often have no such qualms about ridiculing and excluding people with certain disabilities.

THE DISABLED IN NEOLITHIC TIMES

In 2003, archaeologists working on the Buthiers-Boulancourt burial site near Paris, France came across the skeleton of a man whose left arm had been amputated at the elbow. Scar tissue surrounding the cut showed that he had lived as a disabled man. Conventional wisdom and other evidence suggests that at that point in history, those with severe permanent injuries were more often than not abandoned – but this man died of other causes, later, with the full respect of his community. Buried with him were an animal carcass and a large arrowhead, both symbols of prestige.

Ableism: the simplest prejudice

The oldest Paleolithic tools had no handles; they were what their function was. Little consideration was given to the users of a given tool; it was made on the fly to serve a specific function. Some tools were probably kept and reused many times, and others were no doubt discarded and replaced. There was, in any case, no marketplace of tools, so the question was most likely not 'Will someone want to use this?' or 'Will this be comfortable to use?,' but rather 'Will this kill wild game?,' or 'Will this sharpen flint?,' or 'Will this scrape soft tissue from animal bones?' It seems reasonable to assume that if the answer was yes, it was a good tool, and that if the answer was no, it wasn't. Obviously the tools had to be usable, but beyond that there was little adaptive dimension to them.

But at some point in ancient history, the user experience became important. Spears and stone axes were hafted, or attached to handles, which made them easier to use. Atlatls, slingshot-like spear launchers used to hurl them at great velocity, were attached to finger loops so that users could focus more on throwing spears and less on not throwing atlatls. These innovations represent *adaptive* technology – technology that is specifically modified to fit the needs of the user.

And we have, very wisely, continued to adapt technology ever since. Steering wheels are constructed to fit hands with fingers; chairs are generally built so that one can both get into and out of them with relative ease; clothing and shoes are manufactured in a wide range of specific sizes to fit a wide range of specific bodies. But these are seldom custom adaptations, so the manufacturers of these items – who, after all, have to sell them to make a living – create them with certain groups of customers in mind. It's simpler that way.

But as a consequence of this, adaptive technology is very often exclusionary. Women, for example, seldom use urinals. (It's possible to do so, but complicated.) Makeup created for light skin, or hair care products created for straight hair, are not as useful to people who don't have light skin or straight hair. Books written in English are useful only to people who can read English. And so forth.

This gap in accessible tools, tools essential to our everyday lives, can be particularly problematic for the disabled. The blind can never fully access visual media; the deaf can never fully access auditory media; the paralyzed cannot walk or run, and those with severe cognitive difficulties, by definition, find many things to be beyond their comprehension. Some of these limitations are unavoidable. We are all limited in different ways by the bodies and minds that we have.

Indeed, institutional ableism is the only form of systemic discrimination that we are technologically unable to eliminate. Institutional discrimination on the basis of race, nationality, gender, sexual orientation, and gender identity – all of this could be eliminated if sufficient effort were made. But institutional ableism can't be eliminated, because the very definition of a disability is that it prevents us from doing something. Picasso's paintings in a visual medium are inaccessible to the blind, for example, but they aren't inaccessible to the blind because he was insensitive to blind people; they're inaccessible to the blind because it was not within his power to make them otherwise. But if a policy were enacted making it impossible for people of a specific ethnic group or a specific gender to see Picasso's paintings, we would not hesitate to say that the effect was discriminatory, regardless of intent. And the fact that the blind can't see Picasso's paintings is no less discriminatory, even if the discrimination is neither intentional nor human in origin. Some institutional ableism will exist for as long as disabilities are disabilities.

That said, institutional ableism can certainly be *mitigated* – and when people fail to take any reasonable effort to mitigate institutional ableism, the oppression becomes just another form of human discrimination or human bias. The blind can't see Picasso's paintings, but refusing to translate books about Picasso into braille and audio format on the assumption that the blind would not want to read about visual art would constitute unacceptable discrimination. And in the increasingly essential World Wide Web, there is no legitimate reason to make any site inaccessible to people who rely on text-to-speech software. Likewise, there is no legitimate reason to prevent blind people from serving in any occupation that does not actually require sight.

Is 'disability' a medical term?

One of the biggest issues surrounding disability rights is that it's very hard to say what a disability *is*. For example: I have Crouzon Syndrome, an inborn craniofacial malformation that is invariably classified as a disability. It sounds much scarier and more problematic than it actually is. When I was an infant, it was certainly life-threatening – I'm alive and writing this book because I had a good bit of very gruesome-sounding cranial surgery – but today the most life-altering symptom is that my teeth don't line up. Well, plenty of people who don't have Crouzon Syndrome have teeth that don't line up, but most of them would not refer to that as a disability. And while some of my facial features are a little unusual, there are plenty of people whose facial features are much more unusual than mine who don't have a diagnosed craniofacial malformation. So why is it that I get to call myself disabled and they don't? It doesn't seem very fair.

The difference rests in the *medical model* versus the *social model* of disability. According to the medical model, I'm disabled because I have a medical condition – Crouzon Syndrome – that gave me these characteristics. How I feel, how I live, how these characteristics actually affect my life – all of this is secondary to the fact that my characteristics are due to a *disease*, something that physicians can identify as abnormal. People with more severe symptoms who do not have the disease may suffer more, but they're considered *normal* because their symptoms are not considered medical symptoms.

In the disability rights movement, the *social model* of disability tends to be preferred over the medical model. The social model is based on the belief that disability status is determined by society, not by any measurable standard. A good social model of disability, the International Classification of Functioning, was offered up by the World Health Organization (WHO) in 2001. According to the WHO, a disability is 'the outcome of the interaction between a person with an impairment and the environmental and attitudinal barriers he/she may face.'[1] The WHO model is based on the premise that there is no sharp distinction between 'able-bodied' and disabled persons – that we are all, in effect, bozos on this bus. It might be excessively vague (is it really fair to create a definition of disability that assumes that we all agree on what the nearly synonymous term 'impairment' means?), but at least it frames disability status in something other than medical terms.

Thinking about what it really means to be disabled can call into question the very idea of disability status as we have traditionally understood it. If all human beings were blind, for example, then blindness would not be a disability. But would it become a disability if some people were born *with* sight? For that matter, would we all be disabled if some people were born with the capacity for winged flight? Photographic memory is a very useful human trait that very few people possess. So is ambidexterity. Are the rest of us disabled for being born without these traits?

If my friend is too short to reach the top shelf of the supermarket, but she's 5′2″ (1.55m, which most people would not consider to be short enough to constitute a disability), she is certainly affected by non-adaptive technology – but is she really disabled? If another friend is tall enough that sedans are uncomfortable for him, but he's 6′5″ (1.93m, which most people would not consider to be tall enough to constitute a disability), he is certainly affected by non-adaptive technology – but is he really disabled? By any meaningful non-medical standard, we have to say yes. But either would probably laugh if he or she were described as disabled on the basis of his or her height.

I'm not in a position to state definitively what is and is not a disability; nobody is. Fortunately, a rock-solid, permanent definition of disability is not necessary in order to move the agenda of disability rights activism forward. All that is needed is for us to recognize that when anyone is unfairly discriminated against (intentionally or otherwise) due to factors beyond their control, people have a moral obligation to make every reasonable effort to address that discrimination.

Accommodation and discrimination

The disability rights movement is perhaps unique among minority civil rights movements in that it is both unusually large and unusually diverse. According to the UN definition of disability status, approximately one-tenth of the world's population – 650 million people – are classified as disabled;[2] the estimated disabled population of Britain stands at ten million,[3] while the estimated disabled population of the United States stands at fifty million.[4] The disabled include people of both genders and represent all sectors of the ethnic, socioeconomic, religious, and sexual orientation spectra.

Both Britain and the United States prohibit employer discrimination on the basis of disability except in cases where the disability cannot be accommodated, or in cases where the accommodation is too expensive or impractical to implement under current technology. A legal firm cannot refuse to hire or promote an attorney on the basis that she is blind, for example, because reasonable accommodations can be made to allow her to perform her job responsibilities. But there are some occupations for which a blind person is not eligible, given the current state of accommodation technology.

Figure 24 Contestants compete in the Miss Wheelchair Texas pageant. Ableism often excludes those with visible disabilities from mainstream events for which they would otherwise be qualified.

The unemployment rate among the disabled in both Europe and the United States trends high. In Britain, for example, eighty percent of those classified as working age and non-disabled have jobs, compared to fifty percent of those classified as working age and disabled.[5] In the United States, the disparity is even more striking – the national unemployment rate is 4.7 percent, but the unemployment rate for those classified as working age and disabled is forty-four percent.[6] While some disparity between disabled and non-disabled unemployment is to be expected, given that some conditions that classify a person as disabled could make it nearly impossible to work, the majority of disabled working-age Britons and Americans would be able to work full time if not subjected to discrimination and if given an appropriate level of accommodation.

Laws in Britain and the United States also attempt to ensure that public accommodations, including public transportation, be fully accessible to people with disabilities, but in practice this is not generally enforced in a meaningful way. US government authorities lack the staff to investigate complaints under the terms of the Americans with Disabilities Act (ADA), for example, so most instances in which a business has failed to provide adequate access to its facilities under the ADA are either resolved by civil lawsuit (or threat of civil lawsuit), or left unresolved altogether.

Disability rights and HIV-positive status

During the 1980s, as dramatized in the movie *Philadelphia* (1993) starring Tom Hanks, employment discrimination against HIV-positive Americans was rampant. At the time, discrimination was so completely marbled with homophobia that at times it was difficult to tell where the disability discrimination stopped and

---

FEAR ITSELF

In the summer of 2005, forty-three-year-old Claude Green was driving along a Welch, West Virginia road with a friend when he experienced a heart attack. The friend pulled Green out of the car and began performing CPR by the side of the road. Welch police chief Robert K. Bowman showed up and, instead of helping or performing CPR himself, grabbed Green's friend by the shoulders and physically prevented him from continuing CPR. During the ten minutes they waited for paramedics to arrive, Bowman refused to allow anyone to assist Green, who died shortly afterwards. Bowman's reason for letting him die? He believed Green was HIV-positive.

Green was not, in fact, HIV-positive – but he was openly gay, which was good enough for Bowman. And even if Green had been HIV-positive, it is almost impossible to contract HIV by performing CPR under ordinary circumstances.

---

the sexual orientation discrimination began. As HIV has become more visible in all sectors of the population, the discrimination has taken on a character of its own.

In 1998, the US Supreme Court ruled in *Bragdon v. Abbott* that HIV–positive status can be classified as a disability under the Americans with Disabilities Act. As Justice Anthony Kennedy wrote in the 6–3 majority ruling:

> In light of the immediacy with which the virus begins to damage the infected person's white blood cells and the severity of the disease, we hold it is an impairment from the moment of infection. As noted earlier, infection with HIV causes immediate abnormalities in a person's blood, and the infected person's white cell count continues to drop throughout the course of the disease, even when the attack is concentrated in the lymph nodes. In light of these facts, HIV infection must be regarded as

a physiological disorder with a constant and detrimental effect on the infected person's hemic and lymphatic systems from the moment of infection. HIV infection satisfies the statutory and regulatory definition of a physical impairment during every stage of the disease.

But the US Supreme Court's record on HIV discrimination has not been uncheckered. In 2000, the Court refused to hear a challenge to Alabama's prison policies segregating HIV-positive prisoners from the rest of the population, denying the prisoners the level of education, training, and chaplaincy benefits available to non HIV-positive prisoners. The State of Alabama voluntarily ended most of its HIV segregation policies, and granted HIV-positive prisoners greater access to prison facilities, in November 2007.

Figure 25 A sex educator outlines HIV prevention methods to youth peer educators. The Central African Republic has been gravely harmed by the AIDS pandemic.

9
The future of civil liberties

> There is no such thing as the State
> And no one exists alone;
> Hunger allows no choice
> To the citizen or the police;
> We must love one another or die.
>
> (W.H. Auden)[1]

The civil liberties climate has changed a great deal over the past couple of centuries. Of the 193 countries on Earth, 122 are democracies. For the first time in human history, it is hazardous to a country's international reputation to practice overt, policy-based forms of racial discrimination and religious oppression. Not long ago, government officials would have had me killed for writing this book and then have you killed for reading it. We, as a species, have made some progress.

But it isn't necessarily permanent progress, as we learned on April 28, 2004, when photographs of prisoner abuse by US personnel at Abu Ghraib Prison in Baghdad, Iraq began to surface. Suddenly, the United States – touted as the land of the free, the home of the brave, and a leader in international human rights – revealed that no authority, no matter how advanced, is more than a few bad decisions away from creating hell on earth.

Civil liberties are often not just a matter of protecting humanity from those to whom we give power. Sometimes they're a matter of protecting humanity from itself – standing up and establishing ironclad policies and principles now so that we will not be able to violate them easily when the going gets tough. And at other times they are a matter of looking outside of ourselves to find out who we're ignoring, whose civil liberties are *already* being violated.

Both tendencies, to a greater or lesser extent, run counter to our instincts.

Obedience and conformity

In 1961 and 1962, Yale social psychologist Stanley Milgram conducted a now-famous experiment in which a group of men were given a device that, Milgram told them, would deliver electric shocks to a person in the next room. Of the forty subjects in the original experiment, twenty-five repeatedly delivered shocks that they believed went up to 450 volts – despite the audible screams and pleading of the victim – when ordered to do so, based on the victim's incorrect answers on a word-pair test. (The victim was an actor hired by Milgram; nobody was physically harmed in the experiment.) Less commonly known is the fact that, when the experiment was repeated under slightly different circumstances, the rate of obedience was even higher:

> The subject was not ordered to pull the lever that shocked the victim, but merely to perform a subsidiary task (administering the word-pair test) while another person administered the shock. In this situation, thirty-seven of forty adults continued to the highest level of the shock generator. Predictably, they excused their behavior by saying that the responsibility belonged to the man who actually pulled the switch ...
>
> Even Eichmann was sickened when he toured the concentration camps, but he had only to sit at a desk and shuffle papers. At the same time the man in the camp who actually dropped

[Zyklon B] into the gas chambers was able to justify his behavior on the ground that he was only following orders from above. Thus there is a fragmentation of the total human act; no one is confronted with the consequences of his decision to carry out the evil act. The person who assumes responsibility has evaporated.[2]

The Abu Ghraib scandal demonstrates this dynamic perfectly. When Lynndie England was charged with abuse, she blamed Charles Graner. When Charles Graner was charged with abuse, he claimed that he was merely following the directives of his supervisors. When his supervisors were questioned, they claimed that they did not authorize Graner to perform the specific acts that he did. Like all hierarchies, the military chain of command can become a vehicle for accountability or for diffused responsibility. One retired general, speaking on the subject of Abu Ghraib, explained in a 2005 interview:

'The lowest level would be the military guards and intelligence officers in this case. They are held accountable for their personal actions,' says the retired general, who asks that his name not be used because he still works for the Pentagon.

'The second level is supervisory – those people can be held responsible for not only things they've done, but for things they've failed to do.

'The third level is ... the ones who might create an environment that encourages, permits, or tolerates these kinds of activities,' he says.[3]

One question that could also be asked, but seldom is, is why US Southern whites allowed the institution of slavery and racial segregation to continue. A significant contributing factor, in this and other instances of large-scale oppression (the historical problem that inspired Milgram to conduct his study was the Holocaust), is diffused responsibility. Indeed, when people

Figure 26 Abu Ghraib torturer Lynndie England is escorted from the courtroom after being sentenced to three years in prison.

attempt to justify collective civil liberties abuses, they often phrase their arguments in explicit responsibility-diffusion terms. For example:

- 'The Southern way of life,' a phrase used in defense of racial segregation, implies that the responsibility to resolve the issue falls on the South as a whole and that the South as a whole has already decided it. It relieves the individual Southerner of the burden of choice.
- 'Redefining marriage,' a phrase used to dismiss the concept of partnership rights for same-sex couples, implies that the argument has already somehow been resolved by past consensus. It relieves the individual of the burden of choice.

One example of diffused responsibility that is often cited is the Genovese effect. Kitty Genovese, who managed a sports bar in Queens, New York, was on her way home when she was assaulted and repeatedly stabbed by an assailant. Numerous witnesses saw the attack. One apartment resident opened the window and shouted at the assailant, prompting him to flee. Genovese, bleeding but still alive, staggered into an apartment hallway. The assailant later returned and killed her. Although the attack on Genovese lasted more than thirty minutes and was witnessed by thirty-eight people, none of them called the police until after the final attack. Each of the witnesses assumed that the matter was being addressed by others. The story of Genovese is interpreted in many different ways − as an indictment of urban life or contemporary values, or as an indictment of the thirty-eight people who happened to live in that apartment. In light of Milgram's subsidiary-task experiment and similar studies conducted dealing with obedience, it seems to be nothing more than an accurate reflection of what can happen when people, no matter how moral, compassionate, or well intentioned, accept group responsibility and fail to take the initiative.

The idea of diffused responsibility is not new. There is an old Indian story of a leader who demanded that villagers each contribute a certain amount of milk for a religious offering. One villager, who could barely afford the milk and assumed that a glass of water would not noticeably dilute the sacrifice, brought water instead. When he arrived, he found that every-one else had had the same idea − the basin was filled only with water.

But diffused responsibility is seldom a neutral factor, as it was in the case of the Milgram experiment and the death of Kitty Genovese. It can also be a defense mechanism that people use when they *want* to do something that would otherwise be unconscionable. To refer back to the example of white Southern oppression of African-Americans, for example, diffused responsibility allowed the institution to continue – but it also functioned as an internal defense mechanism, allowing whites who were afraid of African-Americans or benefitted from their economic exploitation to maintain a system adapted to their own self-interest.

In many respects, religion can be the ultimate means of responsibility diffusion. By saying that something is God's will, that one's religion dictates it, one can pass on the responsibility for one's actions to a higher power. Televangelist Kenneth Copeland, for example, recently purchased a $20 million private jet with money donated by followers who felt that they were giving money to God. In his book *The Laws of Prosperity*, Copeland writes: 'Do you want a hundredfold return on your money? Give and let God multiply it back to you. No bank in the world offers this kind of return! Praise the Lord!'[4]

If Copeland's argument were framed in non-religious terms, it is difficult to imagine that he could justify the purchase of an expensive private jet based on funds contributed by followers who are in many instances struggling to pay the rent. But by phrasing the argument in religious terms, Copeland can do this; it becomes an act of God and the entire Christian faith. From that perspective, he and those who help administer his televangelism can imagine themselves to be mere vessels put to use by a higher authority – just like the subjects of Milgram's experiments.

Overcoming human nature

The temptation to diffuse responsibility in order to protect one's own way of life, or to advance one's own interests, is not unique to you or me, nor is it even unique to human beings – but it is within our power to control. As Oxford biologist Richard Dawkins wrote in *The Selfish Gene*:

Like successful Chicago gangsters, our genes have survived, in some cases for millions of years, in a highly competitive world. This entitles us to expect certain qualities in our genes ... [and] a predominant quality to be expected in a successful gene is ruthless selfishness. This gene selfishness will usually give rise to selfishness in individual behaviour ...

Be warned that if you wish, as I do, to build a society in which individuals cooperate generously and unselfishly towards a common good, you can expect little help from biological nature. Let us try to teach generosity and altruism, because we are born selfish. Let us understand what our own selfish genes are up to, because we may then at least have the chance to upset their designs.[5]

Civil liberties are often phrased in terms of rational self-interest. People who shoot tend to want gun rights; people who smoke marijuana tend to want to see it legalized; members of oppressed religious groups tend to care very much about religious liberties; same-sex couples tend to support legal protections for same-sex couples. The vast majority of civil liberties movements are organized in this way. And this is to be expected, and this is even to a certain extent noble – there is nothing wrong with acting in one's own self-interest, particularly when it is done in a way that has a positive impact on so many other people.

But when self-interest defines a movement to the point where self-criticism becomes a challenge, blind spots inevitably result. This is why the feminist movement, historically dominated by white heterosexual women, has not historically done enough to incorporate the concerns of lesbians and women of color (though this is beginning to change). This is why it is relatively rare to find someone who is simultaneously concerned about the persecution of Christians, the persecution of Muslims, and the persecution of non-religious persons. As I write this, I am

Figure 27 A member of the US Air Force holds a refugee child from Kabul, Afghanistan.

absolutely certain that there are serious civil liberties concerns that I am not addressing, that I am not taking seriously enough, important civil liberties concerns that in many cases have not even crossed my mind.

That's the nature of civil liberties. As I wrote in the first chapter, tyrants have unlimited civil liberties – and nearly all of us are, relative to some people, tyrants. The species we call *homo sapiens* is a race of oppressors, invaders, and conquerors, the most prolific corpse-eaters in the history of the world. But we have the capacity for empathy, for solidarity, for disobedience, and for love. We have the capacity to see oppression and the capacity to change it. We have seen it. Let's change it.

What you can do

Your liberties and the liberties of those you care about aren't a spectator sport, a parlor game, or an area of academic study. They're serious business. Civil liberties activism is also extremely rewarding – it's a good way to educate yourself on an issue or group of issues, broaden your experience of the world, learn about new issues and goals that resonate with you, and meet new people who share at least some of your values and interests. Internet activism isn't a bad place to start, and it's better than no activism at all, but it isn't as powerful, productive, or socially beneficial as traditional grassroots activism.

This is why reading this book isn't enough. There is no way that any book can tell you everything you need to know about civil liberties. I can give you a good idea of the lay of the land, but a real, visceral understanding of civil liberties means listening firsthand to the stories of people whose civil liberties have

Figure 28 An NAACP activist leads a protest in front of the US Supreme Court building.

been violated. It means understanding what the stakes are. It means understanding why this matters so much. If you're passionate about a specific area of civil liberties, why waste that passion? Find a group and get involved.

I know a few great activists and I've watched them at work. Here's what activism, in my experience, tends to involve.

TEN TIPS FOR CIVIL LIBERTIES ACTIVISM

1 Never trust politicians to do the right thing on their own.
2 Never underestimate the power of a persistent, dedicated, and well-informed constituent.
3 Never underestimate a newcomer's power to become a persistent, dedicated, and informed constituent. It can literally happen overnight.
4 Contagious empathy, kindness, and joy are very effective community-organizing tools.
5 Contagious vindictiveness, hatred, and fatalism are very ineffective community-organizing tools.
6 On particularly controversial topics, it helps to learn to appreciate the arguments against your position. Don't just learn them to debunk them. Learn why people find them inspiring, if in fact people do. Read, ask, listen, and try to keep an open mind.
7 The recipe for a good argument usually works out to two parts emotional connection, one part intellect. This isn't because people are stupid. It is because people care.
8 Be honest. If your argument is based on fudge and spin, then there's a good chance some people will pick up on that and be turned off.
9 Always keep learning, changing, growing.
10 Don't worry about whether or not you're the right person to do a specific kind of activism. If there's work for you to do and it feels like where you need to be, then you've found something worth holding on to.

Listening. I can't stress this highly enough. Listen to the victims of civil liberties violations; then your work will be true to their experiences. Listen to people who are already doing activism in this area; then you'll know what is already being done. Listen to anyone who has something to say, at least up to a point.

Networking. A group of people carrying picket signs on a street corner constitute a protest. One person carrying a picket sign on a street corner all alone might just come across as a weirdo. If there is a movement, find your place in it. Learn where your skills are needed, and what you might be able to do to help.

Community organizing. Networking is what you do when you're trying to get better connected to the movement; organizing is what you do when you're trying to bring people together. Organizing is essential to the growth of activist communities.

Issue advocacy. Persuasion is central to activism. There are many ways to do issue advocacy, from one-on-one conversations to letter-writing campaigns, but all of them benefit if you mentally identify, and relate to, your target audience.

Economic activism. Boycotts and divestments aren't as popular as they used to be, but a sufficiently large-scale, well-organized boycott can still be a useful way to send corporations and governments a message in a language they can understand.

Policy activism. Lobbying legislators and other elected officials can be extremely productive. Face-to-face meetings tend to be more productive than telephone conversations, which tend to be more effective than printed letters, which tend to be more productive than anything Internet based.

Fundraising. Nonprofit organizations always need more money. If you can help bring some of that money in by planning events, it can be used to finance other areas of activism.

Protests. Contrary to conventional wisdom, protesting is not a waste of time. It demonstrates the power of your movement, draws attention to your cause, energizes participants, and gets the attention of local media and elected officials. Entire governments have been toppled by well-organized protests.

Some protests may involve civil disobedience – calculated, intentional violation of unjust laws that essentially recruits police as an activism tool by using arrests, or non-arrests, to garner publicity for the cause.

HOW TO AVOID BURNOUT: FIVE EASY TIPS FOR ACTIVISTS

The two greatest stumbling blocks to civil liberties activism are apathy and burnout. You probably wouldn't be reading this if you were apathetic, so let's focus on burnout. If you get involved in activism, here are five ways that you can ensure it remains a positive experience:

1 **Ask yourself what you're getting out of it**. This may sound like a brutally selfish question, and in a way it is – but miserable activists who hate what they do, and find it emotionally draining, can do more harm than good. As a counterpoint, look at video of any Martin Luther King Jr. speech and you will find a man whose work fed him, energized him, and brought him to life. This was a man who spent time in prison and had to deal with death threats on a daily basis, but there was a contagious sense of joy and purpose to his work that transformed the United States and much of the world. Joy is contagious. Misery is also contagious. Be sure you're spreading the right disease. As the old Erma Bombeck line goes: When you look like your passport photo, it's time to go home.

2 **Try not to burn bridges**. People get worked up when they're doing activism, and sometimes they take it out on the people around them. Try not to get caught up in all of that; it

HOW TO AVOID BURNOUT: FIVE EASY TIPS FOR ACTIVISTS (*cont.*)

produces a negative atmosphere, which is not conducive to getting things done.

3   **Don't commit to more than you can handle.** If you don't have time to do the local web site, say so. If you really don't want to spend hours making phone calls on Christmas Eve, say so. When you volunteer as an activist, you aren't handing over the keys to your life. Along the same lines: It's not usually much fun, or very productive, to run a movement all by yourself. If you can't gather any support for what you're doing, consider working on another issue for a while.

4   **Don't spend all of your activism-related time working with paid staff.** Sooner or later they'll probably leave, and then you'll find yourself among strangers again. Try to work with both paid staff and local volunteers so that your sense of community isn't rocked to the core every time new staff members are hired.

5   **Don't be afraid to try new things.** There is no area of civil liberties activism that *everybody* hates, and there is no area of civil liberties activism that can't use more volunteers – so don't get the idea that you're stuck with a single area of activism just because that's what you've been doing. There are always more causes that need your help. Spend your time with the ones that work for you. As long as you fulfill your existing commitments (see tip 3), you can *always* politely step away and try out something new if you burn out.

Notes

Chapter 1

1. 'Me and Bobby McGee' (1970) was actually written by Kris Kristofferson and Fred Foster, and has been performed by hundreds of musicians (from Johnny Cash to the Grateful Dead), but Janis Joplin's 1971 rendition is usually regarded as the definitive version.

Chapter 2

1. Benjamin Thorpe, editor, *The Anglo-Saxon Chronicle*, London: Longman, Green, Longman, and Roberts, 1861, volume 2, pp. 203–4.
2. Grace Reade Robinson and James Harvey Robinson, editors, *Translations and Reprints from the Original Sources of [European] History*, Philadelphia: University of Pennsylvania Press, 1902, volume 1, pp. 3–4.
3. John Locke, *Two Treatises on Civil Government*, London: Routledge, 1884, pp. 261–2. Originally published in 1689.
4. Thomas Hobbes, *Leviathan*, Oxford: Oxford University Press, 1998, p. 84.
5. Mary Wollestonecraft, *Vindication of the Rights of Woman*, London: Unwin, 1891, p. 100. Originally published in 1792.
6. William W. Brown, *Narrative of William W. Brown: An American Slave*, London: Gilpin, 1849, pp. 136–7.
7. Quoted in 'Great Interviews of the 20th Century: Richard Nixon interviewed by David Frost,' *The Guardian*, September 7, 2007.

Chapter 3

1. The White House, 'Honoring the Victims of the Incidents on Tuesday, September 11, 2001,' September 12, 2001.
2. Quoted in Victor Navasky, 'Profiles in Cowardice,' *The Nation*, October 18, 2001.
3. The White House, Press Briefing by Ari Fleischer, September 26, 2001.
4. Eliza Truitt, 'It's the End of the World as Clear Channel Knows It,' *Slate*, September 17, 2001.
5. Quoted in Newt Gingrich, 'The 1st Amendment is Not a Suicide Pact,' *Human Events*, December 4, 2006.

Chapter 4

1. Edward Norman, quoted in Frank Prochaska, 'The Church of England and the Collapse of Christian Charity,' November 8, 2004. Published by the Social Affairs Unit, and available online: www.socialaffairsunit.org.uk/blog/archives/000207.php
2. Quoted in 'Briefly,' *The Living Church*, May 7, 2000, p. 8.
3. Amnesty International Report 2008, 'People's Republic of China: The crackdown on Falun Gong and other so-called "heretical organizations."' Available online: www.amnesty.org/en/library/asset/ASA17/011/2000/en/dom-ASA170112000en.html
4. Quoted in Conrad Henry Moehlman, *The Wall of Separation Between Church and State: An Historical Study*, Boston: Beacon Press, 1951, p. 14.
5. 'Brigitte Bardot fined £12,000 for racial hatred after claiming Muslims are destroying France,' *Mail Online*, June 3, 2008.
6. Amnesty International, 'Saudi Arabia: Death penalty unfair / unfair trial, Sabri Bogday (M),' April 23, 2008.
7. Dr. M. Younus Shaikh, 'Blasphemy – My Journey Through Hell.' Available online: www.mukto-mona.com/Articles/Younus_Sheikh/blasphemy.htm

8. Ian Fisher and Elisabetta Povoledo, 'Italy Grants Asylum to Afghan Christian Convert,' *The New York Times*, March 30, 2006.

Chapter 5

1. Naomi Klein, 'China's All-Seeing Eye,' *Rolling Stone*, May 29, 2008.
2. Meanwhile, free African-Americans living in the North were often kidnapped by slave traders and sold in the South as slaves – a problem that Southern governments made no serious attempt to address.
3. John Scoffern, *The Philosophy of Common Life*, London: Ward & Lock, 1857, p. 115.
4. Bureau of Justice Statistics, 'Summary findings,' US Department of Justice, December 31, 2006.
5. Duncan Walker, 'How prisons became so busy,' BBC News, April 3, 2006.
6. Aryeh Neier, *Taking Liberties: Four Decades in the Struggle for Rights*, Cambridge, MA: Perseus/PublicAffairs, 2003, pp. 16, 298.
7. Bureau of Justice Statistics, 'Reentry Trends in the U.S.: Recidivism,' US Department of Justice, October 25, 2002.
8. Michael Rempel, Dana Fox-Kralstein, Amanda Cissner, et al., *The New York State Adult Drug Court Evaluation: Policies, Participants and Impacts*, Center for Court Innovation, October 2003, p. 323.
9. Sondra S. Crosby, et al., 'Prevalence of torture survivors among foreign-born patients presenting to an urban ambulatory care practice,' *Journal of General Internal Medicine*, July 2006.
10. The White House, 'President Tours Border, Discusses Immigration Reform in Texas,' November 29, 2005.
11. John Brown Dillon and Ben Douglass, *Oddities of Colonial Legislation in America*, Indianapolis: Douglass, 1879, p. 32.
12. Quoted in Thomas Bender, *Rethinking American History in a Global Age*, Sacramento: University of California Press, 2002, p. 282.

13. The White House, 'President Discusses Creation of Military Commissions to Try Suspected Terrorists,' September 6, 2006.

14. Quoted in Leonard Doyle, 'Waterboarding is torture – I did it myself, says US advisor,' *The Independent*, November 1, 2007.

Chapter 6

1. Human Rights Watch, *Broken People: Caste Violence Against India's 'Untouchables,'* New York: Human Rights Watch, 1999. Chapter I (Summary), paragraphs 20 and 22.

2. 'UN report slams India for caste discrimination,' CBC News, March 2, 2007.

3. Human Rights Watch, *Hidden Apartheid: Caste Discrimination Against India's 'Untouchables,'* New York: Human Rights Watch, 2002. Section I (Summary List), Article 2, paragraphs 1–2.

4. Many sources, including 'Dalit girl burnt in UP,' *The International News* (Pakistan), May 1, 2008.

5. Balwant Garg, 'Dalit youth beaten to death in Moga,' *The Times of India*, June 2, 2008.

6. Prohibition of Forcible Conversion of Religious Ordinance, as signed by P.S. Ramamohan Rao, Governor of Tamil Nadu, October 5, 2002.

7. Nirmala Carvalho, 'Tamil Nadu: A thousand Dalit Christians reconvert to Hinduism,' *Asianews.it*, April 14, 2008.

8. '400 Richest Americans are Billionaires,' *Guardian Unlimited*, September 22, 2006.

9. Aristotle (trans. Peter Simpson), *The Politics*, Book VII, Chapter 7. Chapel Hill: University of North Carolina Press, 1997.

10. David E. Stannard, *American Holocaust: The Conquest of the New World*, New York: Oxford University Press, 1993, p. ix.

11. Ibid., p. x.

12. Joseph Carroll, 'Public Still Supports Path to Citizenship for Illegal Immigrants,' Gallup News Service, March 14, 2007.

13. Quoted in the Commonwealth History Project, '*Rabbit-Proof Fence*: The Question of "Intent" in History.' Published by the National Centre for History Education. Available online: www.hyperhistory.org/index.php?option=displaypage&Itemid=4 55&op=page

14. Jeffrey D. Sachs, 'Welcome to the Asian Century,' *Fortune*, January 12, 2004.

15. Ibid.

16. Benjamin Muindi, 'Africa's economic upsurge vulnerable to shocks,' *Business Daily* (Nairobi), December 6, 2007.

17. Comisión Económica para América Latina y el Caribe, Preliminary overview of the economies of Latin America and the Caribbean 2006, p. 23.

18. Ben Leapman, 'UK "will swell to 75m" as migrant births rise,' *The Telegraph*, October 22, 2007.

19. US Census Bureau, Census 2000 Redistricting (Public Law 94–171) Summary File, Tables PL1 and PL2.

20. US Census Bureau, 2004, 'U.S. Interim Projects by Age, Sex, Race, and Hispanic Origin,' March 18, 2004.

21. Leapman, 'UK "will swell"'.

22. Susan S. Lang, 'Interracial relationships are on the increase in U.S., but decline with age, Cornell study finds,' *Chronicle Online* (Cornell), November 2, 2005.

23. Rob Schmitz, 'Racial profiling study sparks controversy in Rochester,' Minnesota Public Radio, November 18, 2003.

24. Amnesty International USA, 'Testimony from Amnesty International USA's hearings on Racial Profiling,' www.amnestyusa.org/Racial_Profiling

25. Susan Watson and Ash Kosiewicz, 'U.S. Citizen Settles Assault Case Against U.S. Border Patrol Official and U.S. Government,' Texas RioGrande Legal Aid, August 21, 2006.

26. Lee Price, 'Racial discrimination continues to play a part in the hiring process,' *Economic Snapshots* (Economic Policy Institute), September 17, 2003.

27. 'French Muslims face job discrimination,' BBC News, November 2, 2005.

28. Lorinda M. Bullock, '"Linguistic Profiling" of Katrina Survivors,' *The Louisiana Weekly*, August 7, 2006.

Chapter 7

1. Sheila Thomas, 'Intersectionality: The Double Bind of Race and Gender,' *Perspectives*, Spring 2004.

2. R. Scott Moxley, 'Unreasonable Doubts,' *OC Weekly*, July 1, 2004; Larry Welborn and Rachanee Srisavasdi, 'Haidl, co-defendants get 6 years each,' *OC Register*, March 11, 2006.

3. Frances Harrison, 'Saudi rape victim is jailed,' BBC News, November 15, 2007.

4. Amnesty International, 'Doubly Traumatized: Lack of access to justice for female victims of sexual and gender-based violence in northern Uganda,' November 30, 2007.

5. Michael Holden, 'Rape trial plans to boost convictions,' Reuters, November 28, 2007.

6. The Commonwealth Fund, 'Health Concerns Across a Woman's Lifespan: 1998 Survey of Women's Health,' May 1999.

7. The White House, 'National Domestic Violence Awareness Month: A Proclamation,' October 1, 2002.

8. Sex Offenses and Offenders, Bureau of Justice Statistics, US Department of Justice, February 1997.

9. National Crime Victimization Survey, Bureau of Justice Statistics, US Department of Justice, 2000.

10. Hart and Rennison, Bureau of Justice Statistics Special Report, US Department of Justice, 2003. Quoted by St. Lawrence University, Student Advocate Program, www.stlawu.edu/advocates/women_of_color_stats.php

11. Terri Henry, 'Tribal Response to Violence Against Women,' 1998 Presentation to the Federal Bar Association Conference, Indian Law Division. Quoted by St. Lawrence University, Student Advocate Program.

12. US Code, Title IX, Section 1681.

13. US Federal Register, Volume 69, Number 46, March 9, 2004, p. 11279.

14. Monica Langley, 'Friends of Hillary,' *The Wall Street Journal,* December 8, 2007.

15. 'Women in Parliament,' BBC News, January 26, 2006.

16. James Westhead, 'Women power comes to Capitol Hill,' BBC News, January 2, 2007.

17. Kristine Nergaard, 'Rules on minimum gender representation on company boards come into force,' European Foundation for the Improvement of Living and Working Conditions, February 23, 2006.

18. W.H.D. Rouse, translator, *The Iliad* of Homer, New York: Signet, 1999, pp. 43, 77.

19. Aubery de Selincourt, translator, *The Histories* of Herodotus, New York: Penguin, 2003, pp. 277–8.

20. Claire Smith, 'The sex lives of Scotland's children,' *The Scotsman*, March 24, 2005.

21. Sey Chassler, 'Teenage Girls Talk About Pregnancy,' *PARADE*, February 2, 1997. Quoted in the National Campaign to Prevent Teen and Unplanned Pregnancy, 'What the Polling Data Tells Us: A Summary of Past Surveys on Teen Pregnancy,' April 1997.

22. Laura Sessions Stepp, 'A New Kind of Date Rape,' *Cosmopolitan*, September 2007.

23. Chassler, 'Teenage Girls.'

24. EDK Associates for *seventeen* magazine and the Ms. Foundation for Women, *Teenagers Under Pressure*, 1996. Quoted in ibid.

25. Elisabeth Rosenthal, 'Legal or not, abortion rates similar,' *International Herald Tribune*, October 11, 2007.

26. 'An Overview of Clandestine Abortion in Latin America,' Guttmacher Institute, December 1996.

27. L. B. Finer et al., 'Reasons U.S. women have abortions: quantitative and qualitative perspectives,' *Perspectives on Sexual and Reproductive*

Health, 2005. Quoted in 'Facts on Induced Abortion in the United States,' The Guttmacher Institute, May 2006.

28. Louisa Lim, 'Cases of Forced Abortions Surface in China,' National Public Radio (United States), April 23, 2007.

Chapter 8

1. Quoted in Disabled Peoples' International (DPI), 'DPI Position Paper on the Definition of Disability,' May 19, 2005.
2. 'Disability pact passes UN panel,' Reuters, August 25, 2006.
3. 'Updated estimate of the number of disabled people including people with limiting longstanding illnesses, and their associated spending power,' Department for Work and Pensions (UK), February 9, 2006.
4. 'Disability and the 2000 Census: What reporters need to know,' the Center for an Accessible Society, www.accessiblesociety.org/topics/demographics-identity/census2000.htm
5. Office for National Statistics (UK), *Labour Force Survey*, September to December, 2006. Quoted in 'Disability and employment statistics,' Shaw Trust, www.shaw-trust.org.uk/page/6/89/
6. Audrey Reed, 'People with disabilities make up largest job-seeking minority group,' *Inland Valley Daily Bulletin*, December 9, 2007.

Chapter 9

1. W. H. Auden, 'September 1, 1939.' Some versions substitute 'We must love one another and die.'
2. Stanley Milgram, 'The Perils of Obedience,' *Harper's Magazine*, December 1973.
3. Faye Bowers, 'Abu Ghraib's Message for the Rank and File,' *The Christian Science Monitor*, May 6, 2005.
4. Kenneth Copeland, *The Laws of Prosperity*, Fort Worth, TX: Kenneth Copeland Publications, 1995, p. 67.
5. Richard Dawkins, *The Selfish Gene*, 2nd edition, Oxford University Press, 1989, pp. 2–3.

Recommended reading

Books

Civil Liberties and Human Rights, 4th edition, Helen Fenwick, Routledge Cavendish, 2007.

Civil Liberties and Human Rights in England and Wales, 2nd edition, David Feldman, Oxford University Press, 2002.

Cyber Rights: Defending Free Speech in the Digital Age, revised edition, Mike Godwin, MIT Press, 2003.

The Decency Wars: The Campaign to Cleanse American Culture, Frederick S. Lane, Prometheus, 2006.

The First Freedom: A History of Free Speech, Robert Hargreaves, Sutton, 2002.

From Secularism to Jihad: Sayyid Qutb and the Foundations of Radical Islamism, Adnan A. Musallam, Praeger, 2005.

The Future of Freedom: Illiberal Democracy at Home and Abroad, revised edition, Fareed Zakaria, Norton, 2007.

Hiding From Humanity: Disgust, Shame, and the Law, Martha Nussbaum, Princeton, 2004.

In Defense of Our America: The Fight for Civil Liberties in the Age of Terror, Anthony D. Romero and Dina Temple-Raston, HarperCollins, 2007.

More Secure, Less Free?: Antiterrorism Policy and Civil Liberties After 9/11, Mark Sidel, University of Michigan Press, 2007.

Roger Nash Baldwin and the American Civil Liberties Union, Robert Cottrell, Columbia University Press, 2001.

Sin No More: From Abortion to Stem Cells, Understanding Crime, Law, and

Morality in America, John Dombrick and Daniel Hillyard, NYU Press, 2007.

The Torture Papers: The Road to Abu Ghraib, Karen J. Greenberg and Joshua L. Dratel, eds, Cambridge, 2005.

Toward an Islamic Reformation: Civil Liberties, Human Rights, and International Law, Abdullahi Ahmed An-Naim, Syracuse University Press, 1996.

The Triumph of Liberty: A 2,000 Year History Told Through the Lives of Freedom's Greatest Champions, Jim Powell, Free Press, 2000.

Your Rights: The Liberty Guide to Human Rights, 8th edition, Megan Addis and Penelope Morrow, Pluto Press, 2005.

Blogs

Action on Rights for Children – http://archrights.wordpress.com/

American Civil Liberties Union, ACLU Blog of Rights – http://blog.aclu.org

Amnesty International, Amnesty USA Blogs – http://blogs.amnestyusa.org

Big Brother State – http://bigbrotherstate.blogspot.com/

Can't Stop Won't Stop – www.cantstopwontstop.com/blog/index.cfm

Capital Defense Weekly – www.capitaldefenseweekly.com

The Cato Institute, Cato @ Liberty – http://www.cato-at-liberty.org/

Danger Room – http://blog.wired.com/defense

The Disloyal Opposition – www.tuccille.org/blog

Drug Policy Alliance, The D'Alliance – http://blog.drugpolicy.org

Gay Rights Watch – http://blog.gayrightswatch.com

Tom Head, About.com: Civil Liberties – http://civilliberty.about.com (full disclosure: I am the author of this blog)

Elisa Mason, Forced Migration Current Awareness Blog – http://fm-cab.blogspot.com

Privacy Digest – www.privacydigest.com

Reason Magazine, Hit & Run – www.reason.com/blog

Samizdata – www.samizdata.net/blog

SCOTUSblog – www.scotusblog.com/wp

Chris Songhoian, Surveill@nce St@te – http://news.cnet.com/
surveillance-state/

SpyBlog – www.spy.org.uk

UK Liberty – http://ukliberty.wordpress.com/

UNICEF Field Notes – http://fieldnotes.unicefusa.org

The Volokh Conspiracy – www.volokh.com

Civil liberties and human rights organizations

This directory is largely limited to organizations that have Internet web sites in English. If you're interested in civil liberties activism in a specific country not listed here, contact an international or regional human rights organization for more specific resources.

International and Regional Organizations

African Commission on Human and Peoples' Rights (ACHPR)

48 Kairaba Avenue, PO Box 673
Banjul
The Gambia
Phone: +220 (43) 92962 / +220 (43) 72070 / +220 (43) 77721
Fax: +220 (43) 90764
Email: achpr@achpr.org
Web: www.achpr.org

Addresses a broad spectrum of human rights and civil liberties issues in Africa, and networks with local and ad hoc organizations to promote same.

Amnesty International

International Secretariat
1 Easton Street
London WC1X 0DW
UK
Phone: +44 (20) 7413 5500
Fax: +44 (20) 7956 1157
Web: www.amnesty.org

Amnesty International (AI) is arguably the world's leading human rights organization. While its most visible driving focus has been on the rights of dissident prisoners, it has also worked to abolish capital punishment, end racist and sexist policy practices, protect the rights to free speech and free religious expression, and otherwise protect the oppressed from governments that would do them harm. The organization investigates, reports on, and (wherever possible) conducts local activism in every country on Earth – including yours – so if you don't see another organization that interests you listed here, contact AI. They'll know what to do.

European Civil Liberties Network (ECLN)

Email: info@ecln.org
Web: www.ecln.org

A new organization addressing civil liberties issues throughout Europe.

Human Rights Foundation

350 Fifth Avenue, #809
New York, NY 10118
USA
Phone: +1 (212) 246 8486
Fax: +1 (212) 643 4278
Email: info@thehrf.org
Web: www.thehrf.org

Addresses human rights and civil liberties issues in the Americas.

Human Rights Watch

350 Fifth Avenue, 34th Floor
New York, NY 10118–3299
USA
Phone: +1 (212) 290 4700
Fax: +1 (212) 736 1300
Email: hrwnyc@hrw.org
Web: www.hrw.org

Cofounded by former American Civil Liberties Union executive director Aryeh Neier, HRW functions as a newer and more US-based counterpart to Amnesty International (with five US chapters and additional chapters in six other countries). HRW is smaller than AI, but it has its own unique advantages – an excellent history of publishing useful research material for advocacy purposes, and a solid commitment to a comprehensive approach to human rights. If you're interested in international human rights and civil liberties but do not feel at home with AI, HRW may be for you.

MADRE: An International Women's Human Rights Organization

121 West 27th Street, #301
New York, NY 10001
USA
Phone: +1 (212) 627 0444
Fax: +1 (212) 675 3704
Email: madre@madre.org
Web: www.madre.org

Addresses global human rights issues, organized by region. Focuses primarily on women, children, and the elderly.

Open Society Institute (OSI)

400 West 59th Street
New York, NY 10019

USA
Phone: +1 (212) 548 0600
Web: www.soros.org
Global charity established by George Soros to encourage the formation and preservation of open societies.

Armenia
The Civil Society Institute

Aygestan 11th Str, 43 Building
Yerevan, Armenia
Phone: +374 (10) 574 317
Email: csi@csi.am
Web: www.csi.am/eng

Australia
Civil Liberties Australia (CLA)

PO Box 7438
Fisher Act 2611
Australia
Web: www.cla.asn.au

New South Wales Council for Civil Liberties

PO Box 201
Glebe NSW 2037
Australia
Phone: +61 (02) 9660 7582
Fax: +61 (02) 9566 4162
Email: office@nswccl.org.au
Web: www.nswccl.org.au

Bahrain

Bahrain Center for Human Rights (BCHR)

Email: info@bahrainrights.org
Web: www.bahrainrights.org

Bahrain Youth Society for Human Rights (BYSHR)

Web: www.byshr.org

Bangladesh

Human Rights Congress for Bangladesh Minorities (HRCBM)

PO Box 5493
Santa Clara, CA 95056–5493
USA
Email: info@hrcbm.org
Web: www.hrcbm.org

Bosnia and Herzegovina

The Helsinki Committee for Human Rights in Bosnia and Herzegovina

Ante Fijamenga 14b
71000 Sarajevo
Bosna i Hercegovina
Phone: +387 (33) 660 809
Email: info@bh-hchr.org
Web: www.bh-hchr.org

Botswana

Ditshwanelo: The Botswana Centre for Human Rights

Private Bag 00416
Gaborone
Botswana
Phone: +267 (62) 52473
Email: admin.ditshwanelo@info.bw
Web: www.ditshwanelo.bw

Burma

The Burma Campaign

28 Charles Square
London N1 6HT
England
Phone: +44 (20) 7324 4710
Fax: +44 (20) 7324 4717
Email: info@burmacampaign.org.uk
Web: www.burmacampaign.org.uk

Cambodia

Cambodian Center for Human Rights

House No. 798
St 99
Boeung Trabek
Phnom Penh
Kingdom of Cambodia
Phone: +855 (23) 726 901
Fax: +855 (23) 726 902
Email: info@ccrhr-cambodia.org
Web: www.ccrhr-cambodia.org

Canada
Canadian Civil Liberties Association (CCLA)

506–360 Bloor Street West
Toronto, ON M5S 1X1
Canada
Phone: +1 (416) 363 0321
Fax: +1 (416) 861 1291
Email: mail@ccla.org
Web: www.ccla.org

China
Human Rights in China

350 Fifth Avenue, Suite 3311
New York, NY 10118
USA
Phone: +1 (212) 239 4495
Fax: +1 (212) 239 2561
Email: hrichina@hrichina.org
Web: www.hrichina.org

Colombia
Colombia Support Network

PO Box 1505
Madison, WI 53701
USA
Phone: +1 (608) 257 8753
Fax: +1 (608) 255 6621
Email: csn@igc.org
Web: www.colombiasupport.net

Denmark

The Danish Institute for Human Rights

Strandgade 56
1401 Copenhagen K
Denmark
Phone: +45 (32) 698 888
Fax: +45 (32) 698 800
Email: center@humanrights.dk
Web: www.humanrights.dk

Egypt

The Egyptian Organization for Human Rights

8/10 Mathaf El-Manial St
10th Floor
Manyal El-roda, Cairo
Egypt
Phone: +20 (2) 363 6811
Fax: +20 (2) 362 1613
Web: en.eohr.org

Eritrea

Eritrean Movement for Democracy and Human Rights

Esselen 171
Sunnyfair Office Blocks, 3rd Floor
Office Number 302, 303, 304
Sunnyside, Pretoria
Gauteng
Republic of South Africa
Phone: +27 (12) 440 4749
Web: www.emdhr.org

Ethiopia

Ethiopian Human Rights Council

PO Box 2432
Addis Ababa
Ethiopia
Phone: +251 (15) 514 489
Email: ehrco@ethionet.et
Web: www.ehrco.org

Guatemala

Guatemala Human Rights Commission (GHRC)/USA

3321 12th Street, NE
Washington, DC 20017
Phone: +1 (202) 529 6599
Fax: +1 (202) 526 4611
Email: ghrc-usa@ghrc-usa.org
Web: www.ghrc-usa.org

Haiti

Institute for Justice and Democracy in Haiti (IJDH)

PO Box 745
Joseph, OR 97846
USA
Phone: +1 (541) 432 0597
Fax: +1 (541) 432 0264
Web: www.ijdh.org
Email: info@ijdh.org

A US-based organization, largely Haitian-run, which focuses on human rights issues impacting Haitian communities. In addition to its own advocacy and organizing work, IJDH funds the Bureau des Avocats Internationaux (BAI) in Port-au-Prince, a group of lawyers pursuing human rights cases in Haiti.

Hungary

Hungarian Human Rights Foundation

PO Box J, Gracie Station
New York, NY 10028
USA
Phone: +1 (212) 289 5488
Fax: +1 (212) 996 6268
Email: hamos@hhrf.org
Web: www.hhrf.org

India

Coimbatore Human Rights Forum

Door No: 23/1, Govt Arts College Road
Coimbatore – 641 018
Tamil Nadu
India
Phone: +91 (42) 2439 4101
Fax: +91 (42) 2437 7125
Email: chrfindia@hotmail.com
Web: geocities.com/humanrights_cbe

People's Union for Civil Liberties

81 Sahayoga Apartments
Mayur Vihar – I
Delhi 110091
India
Phone: +91 (11) 2275 0014
Fax: +91 (11) 2275 7694
Email: national@pucl.org
Web: www.pucl.org

Indonesia
TAPOL

111 Northwood Road
Thornton Heath
Surrey CR7 8HW
England
Phone: +44 (20) 8771 2904
Fax: +44 (20) 8653 0322
Email: tapol@gn.apc.org
Web: tapol.gn.apc.org

Iran
Mission for Establishment of Human Rights in Iran (MEHR)

PO Box 2037
PVP, CA 90274
USA
Phone: +1 (310) 377 4590
Fax: +1 (310) 377 3103
Email: mehr@mehr.org
Web: www.mehr.org

Ireland
Irish Council for Civil Liberties (ICCL)

DMG Business Centre
9–13 Blackhall Place
Dublin 7
Ireland
Phone: +353 (1) 799 4500
Email: info@iccl.ie
Web: www.iccl.ie

Israel and Occupied Territories
The Association for Civil Rights in Israel (ACRI)

PO Box 34510
Jerusalem 91000
Israel
Phone: +972 (2) 652 1218
Fax: +972 (2) 652 1219
Email: mail@acri.org.il
Web: www.acri.org.il

Japan
Japan Civil Liberties Union (JCLU)

306 Atagoyama Bengoshi Building
1–6–7 Atago, Minato-ku
Tokyo
Japan
Phone: +81 (3) 3437 6989
Fax: +81 (3) 3578 6687
Email: jclu@jclu.org
Web: www.jclu.org

Kenya
Kenya Human Rights Commission (KHRC)

Gitanga Road opp. Valley Arcade Shopping Center
PO Box 41079–00100
Nairobi
Kenya
Phone: +254 (20) 387 4998
Fax: +254 (20) 387 4997
Email: admin@khrc.or.ke
Web: www.khrc.or.ke

Laos
Hmong Lao Human Rights Council

Web: www.laohumanrightscouncil.org

Latvia
Latvian Centre for Human Rights (LCHR)

13 Alberta Street
7th Floor
Riga LV-1010
Latvia
Phone: +371 (70) 39290
Fax: +371 (70) 39291
Email: office@humanrights.org.lv
Web: www.humanrights.org.lv

Lebanon
Institute for Human Rights, Lebanon

Beirut Bar Association
Court House
Beirut
Lebanon
Phone: +961 (1) 422 204
Fax: +961 (1) 423 943
Email: idh@inco.com.lb
Web: www.humanrightslebanon.org

Macedonia
Macedonian Human Rights Movement International (MHRMI)

157 Adelaide Street West, Suite 434
Toronto, Canada M5H 4E7

Phone: +1 (416) 850 7125
Fax: +1 (416) 850 7127
Email: info@mhrmi.org
Web: www.mhrmi.org

Malawi
Malawi Human Rights Commission

H.B. House
Private Bag 378, Capital City
Lilongwe 3
Malawi
Phone: +265 (1) 750 900
Fax: +265 (1) 750 943
Email: info@malawihrc.org
Web: www.malawihumanrightscommission.org

Namibia
National Society for Human Rights

Liberty Center
116 John Meinert Street, Corner of Schoenlein Street
Windhoek West
PO Box 23592
Windhoek
Namibia
Phone: +264 (61) 236 183
Fax: +264 (61) 234 286
Email: nshr@nshr.org.na
Web: www.nshr.org.na

Nepal
Alliance for Democracy and Human Rights in Nepal (ADHRN)

Phone: +1 (718) 575 9385
Email: adhrn@alliancenepal.org
Web: www.alliancenepal.org

Nigeria
Human Rights and Justice Group

53 Western Avenue
Ojuelegba, Surulere 101014
Lagos
Nigeria
Phone: +234 (08) 0392 3400
Email: info@justicegroup.org
Web: www.justicegroup.org

Pakistan
Pakistan International Human Rights Organization

#12, 1-D, 2nd Floor, Rahmat Plaza
Nazim-ud-Din Road
Blue Area, Islamabad
Pakistan
Phone: +92 (51) 282 8791
Fax: +92 (51) 287 2092
Email: info@pihro.org
Web: www.pihro.org

Qatar
National Human Rights Committee

PO Box 24104
Doha
Qatar
Phone: +974 444 4012
Fax: +974 444 4013
Email: nhrc@qatar.org.qa
Web: www.nhrc.org.qa

South Africa
Lawyers for Human Rights

Kutlwanong Democracy Centre
357 Visagie Street
Pretoria 0002
South Africa
Phone: +27 (12) 320 2943
Fax: +27 (12) 320 2949
Web: www.lhr.org.za

Sweden
Raoul Wallenberg Institute of Human Rights and Humanitarian Law

Stora Grabrödersg, 17B
PO Box 1155
SE-221 05
Lund
Sweden
Phone: +46 (46) 222 1200
Fax: +46 (46) 222 1222
Web: www.rwi.lu.se

Syria

National Organization for Human Rights in Syria (NOHR-S)

Web: www.nohr-s.org

Taiwan

Taiwan Association for Human Rights (TAHR)

Email: tahr@seed.net.tw
Web: www.tahr.org.tw

Uganda

Human Rights Uganda

Web: www.humanrightsuganda.org

United Kingdom

National Council for Civil Liberties

21 Tabard Street
London SE1 4LA
England
Phone: +44 (20) 7403 3888
Web: www.liberty-human-rights.org.uk

United States

American Civil Liberties Union (ACLU)

125 Broad Street, 18th Floor
New York, NY 10004
USA
Web: www.aclu.org

Vietnam

Vietnam Human Rights Network

14550 Magnolia Street, Suite 203
Westminster, CA 92683
USA
Phone: +1 (714) 897 1950
Email: vnhrnet@vietnamhumanrights.net
Web: www.vietnamhumanrights.net

Zimbabwe

Zimbabwe Human Rights Associations (ZimRights)

90 Fourth Street
Harare
Zimbabwe
Phone: +263 (4) 705 898
Web: www.zimrights.co.zw

Glossary of terms

Accommodationism   On church–state issues, the position that the government need not observe a wall of separation of church and state, but must support (or accommodate) all religions equally. For more on accommodationism, see chapter 4. Accommodationism is one of three major positions on church–state issues, representing a middle ground between *preferentialism* and *separationism*.

Advocacy   The work of convincing people to change or strengthen their views on a given issue, or to convince people to take action. For more on advocacy, see chapter 9.

Anarchism   The position that government, at least in its traditional form, is unnecessary and detrimental. During the early twentieth century, anarchism was viewed as the biggest danger to Western national security interests. Following the 1916 Russian revolution, fear of socialism began to replace fear of anarchism; and following the collapse of the Soviet Union in 1991, fear of *Islamism* began to replace fear of socialism.

Apartheid   An intentional policy of segregation. Racial apartheid was the name given to the policy of segregation adopted by the South African government, but the term is just as applicable to the pre-desegregation United States. For more on racial apartheid, see chapter 6. The term 'gender apartheid' is also sometimes used to describe segregation between the sexes, as described in chapter 7.

Big Brother   The name given to the mysterious (and perhaps fictitious) all-powerful government leader described in George

Orwell's seminal novel *Nineteen Eighty-Four* (1948), which describes a *fascist dystopia* called Oceania. In common parlance, it is used as a derogatory term to refer to, and personalize, government power.

Blasphemy   Speech, writing, or other media that are offensive to religious sensibilities. Laws against blasphemy are extremely common in the Muslim world, and were once extremely common in the West as well. Blasphemy was technically illegal in England and Wales, for example, until May 2008. For more about blasphemy laws, see chapter 4.

Caste   A unit of intentional class segregation based on birthright. The term is most commonly used to refer to India's caste system, but can be used to describe many other systems that attempt to establish class hierarchies. For more about castes, see chapter 6.

Chattel slavery   Slavery that classifies an individual as property, usually from birth. This can be distinguished from *indentured servitude*, a form of slavery based on an unpaid debt or another potentially less permanent condition. For more about slavery, see chapter 6.

Christian Dominionism   An extreme *preferentialist* and *theocratic* view that the Christian Bible, as interpreted by some fundamentalists, should form the basis of government rather than a secular constitution. Christian Dominionists often advocate (among other things) death by stoning for accused blasphemers, adulterers, and gay men. For more about Christian Dominionism, see chapter 4.

Cisgender   A cisgender person is someone who identifies fully as a member of their assigned gender, while *transgender* persons do not. For more on cisgender and transgender persons, see chapter 7.

Civil disobedience An intentional illegal but nonviolent action committed in protest against unjust laws. For more on civil disobedience, see chapter 9.

Closed society A society in which the government exercises strict control over personal liberty and the flow of information; the opposite of an *open society*. For more on open and closed societies, see chapter 2.

COINTELPRO A program of the US Federal Bureau of Investigation, conducted from 1956 to 1971, in which government agents spied on and infiltrated protest groups in an effort to undermine them. Targets of COINTELPRO ranged from civil rights activists such as Martin Luther King Jr. to white supremacist groups such as the Ku Klux Klan. For more on COINTELPRO, see chapter 5.

Community organizing Movement-building. Activism that involves increasing the number of participants, and the level of participation, in a meaningful activist movement, usually one that focuses on issues that directly affect the majority of the participants. For more on community organizing, see chapter 9.

Conservatism As historically defined, a political philosophy that focuses primarily on traditions and existing social structures rather than philosophical arguments and social reform – but the meaning of the term has become more nebulous over time. Contemporary subcategories of conservatism include paleoconservatism and neoconservatism. A counterpoint, but not a direct opposite to, *liberalism*. For more on conservatism, see chapter 1.

Cultural feminism The position that men and women think and deal with the world in fundamentally different ways that are rooted in biology rather than culture, that activism is of limited value, and that *institutional sexism* can only be effectively avoided by establishing separate women's power systems in which men, who for biological reasons cannot help but promote patriarchy, do not participate. Cultural feminism is distinguished from *liberal feminism*, which emphasizes policy reform, and *radical feminism*, which challenges rather than affirms traditional notions of gender difference. For more on cultural feminism, see chapter 7.

Dalit 'Untouchable.' An outcast in the Indian *caste* system, often relegated to poverty and especially demeaning kinds of manual labor. For more on the Indian caste system, see chapter 6.

Despotism A government ruled by one or more *despots*, leaders who have obtained and retain power entirely by force or the threat of force. For more on despotism, see chapter 1.

Diaspora Large-scale emigration of an ethnic, cultural, or religious group from a geographic region. Two commonly cited examples are the African diaspora, caused by the Atlantic slave trade, and the Jewish diaspora, caused by imperial conquest and subjugation of Israel. For more on diasporas, see chapter 6.

Dystopia A horrible world or nation envisioned and described as a cautionary tale. The opposite of a *utopia*. For more about utopias and dystopias, see chapter 1.

ECHELON A system established jointly by the Australian, Canadian, New Zealand, UK, and US governments to monitor some satellite transmissions and other unknown international communications for national security purposes. For more on ECHELON, see chapter 5.

Fascism A system of government that is hyper-nationalistic, hyper-authoritarian, usually formed to appeal to a *utopian* principle. For more about fascism, see chapter 1.

Fighting words Words that do not generally receive free speech protection because they are spoken or shouted in a context where they are clearly intended to promote violence and/or other forms of disorder. Following a stranger on the sidewalk while shouting racial epithets, for example, is not generally considered a form of protected free speech. For more on fighting words, see chapter 3.

Foreign Intelligence Surveillance Act (FISA)   Legislation passed by the US Congress in 1978 to limit the president's power to conduct surveillance on the purported basis of national security. In 2008, FISA was weakened considerably by new amendments. For more on FISA, see chapter 5.

Genocide   The successful or attempted extermination of an entire racial or ethnic group within national borders. A form of ethnic cleansing. For more on genocide, see chapter 6.

Habeas corpus   Latin: 'You have the body.' The basic right of a prisoner to challenge his or her imprisonment in an impartial court of law. For more on *habeas corpus*, see chapter 5.

Heteronormativity   The promotion of heterosexual rights, practices, and relationships over gay and lesbian rights, practices, and relationships. For more on heteronormativity, see chapter 7.

Indecent   Offensive to community sensibilities, but not necessarily *obscene*. For more on indecency and obscenity, see chapter 3.

Indentured servitude   A form of slavery in which forced labor is used to pay off debts. For more on slavery, see chapter 6.

Institutional racism   A term coined by civil rights activist Stokely Carmichael to refer to the racist effects of societal practices, as opposed to individual racist behavior. For more on institutional racism, see chapter 6.

Institutional sexism   A term, inspired by Carmichael's concept of *institutional racism*, used to refer to the sexist effects of societal practices as opposed to individual sexist behavior. For more on institutional sexism, see chapter 7.

International Criminal Court An international tribunal established by members of the United Nations to prosecute crimes against humanity. For more on the International Criminal Court, see chapter 2.

Intersectionality The combined effects of multiple forms of personal or institutional prejudice on a person who falls into more than one category of oppression. A black lesbian, for example, is affected in an intersectional way by heteronormativity, racism, and sexism. For more on intersectionality, see chapter 7.

Islamism An extreme *preferentialist* and *theocratic* view that Islamic theology and *Sharia* law, as interpreted by some fundamentalists, should form the basis of government rather than a secular constitution. Advocates of Islamism often advocate (among other things) death by stoning for accused blasphemers, adulterers, and gay men. For more about Islamism, see chapter 4.

Jim Crow A system of *apartheid* established by state governments in the American South in the aftermath of World War II as a means of promoting *institutional racism*. For more on Jim Crow, see chapter 6.

Liberal feminism The view that *institutional sexism* can best be addressed through calculated, achievable policy reform. Liberal feminism can be distinguished from *cultural feminism*, which tends to question the value of activism, and *radical feminism*, which seeks dramatic cultural change. For more on liberal feminism, see chapter 7.

Liberalism As historically defined, a political philosophy that focuses primarily on philosophical arguments and social reform rather than traditions and existing social structures – but the meaning of the term has become more nebulous over time. A counterpoint, but not a direct opposite to, *conservatism*. For more on liberalism, see chapter 1.

Libertarianism   A vaguely defined umbrella term that can be used to describe any political philosophy that emphasizes reducing the power and scope of government. A less extreme alternative to *anarchism*. Proponents of both *conservatism* and *liberalism* often claim to be libertarians. For more on libertarianism, see chapter 1.

Lobbying   An attempt to use direct *advocacy* to influence policymakers' decisions. Often vilified, lobbying is a crucial part of every liberal democracy. For more on lobbying, see chapter 9.

Milgram experiments   A series of experiments conducted by Yale psychologist Stanley Milgram during the 1960s and 1970s to measure the average person's ability to resist unethical commands delivered by authority figures. In *Obedience to Authority* (1974), Milgram summarized his findings – which demonstrated that blind obedience is a distressingly common trait. For more on the Milgram experiments, see chapter 9.

Moderate physical pressure   Relatively mild forms of torture permitted at one point by the Israeli government, and later adopted by the US government following the terrorist attacks of September 11, 2001. For more on moderate physical pressure and other torture techniques, see chapter 5.

Nativism   The promotion of the interests of the native-born population over the rights and/or interests of immigrants, often accompanied by *xenophobia*. For more on nativism, see chapter 6.

Natural rights   In philosophy, the rights to which every person is entitled at birth according to God and/or the natural order of things. For more on natural rights, see chapter 1.

Negative liberty   Freedom from direct government interference. Often viewed in tension with *positive liberty*, though the two goals are not always mutually exclusive (as either can be used either to expand or reduce the amount of *real liberty*). Negative liberty is often associated with *libertarianism* and some forms of paleoconservatism, but negative liberty with respect to personal behavior is also highly valued in *liberalism*. For more on negative liberty, see chapter 1.

Obscene   Material that is so graphic and offensive to community standards, and so devoid of any apparent artistic, scientific, historical, or literary value, that the government considers it outside of the realm of free speech protections. Almost exclusively used to describe pornography. Can be distinguished from *indecent* material, which is offensive to community standards but protected by free speech laws. For more on obscenity, see chapter 3.

Open society   A society in which the government permits a high degree of personal liberty and does not strictly control the flow of information; the opposite of a *closed society*. For more on open and closed societies, see chapter 2.

Orwellian   A government or government policy that is so offensive to one's standards of personal liberty that it is reminiscent of the policies enacted in the name of *Big Brother* in the *dystopia* described in George Orwell's novel *Nineteen Eighty-Four* (1948).

Positive liberty   The constructive use of government power to increase personal freedom. An example of a policy that promotes positive liberty might be a law prohibiting employment discrimination on the basis of race. While it technically reduces the *negative liberty* of employers to make human resources decisions based on whatever criteria they consider appropriate, it also substantially enhances the *positive liberty* of members of minority groups. For more on positive liberty, see chapter 1.

Preferentialism   On church–state issues, the position that the government need not observe a wall of separation of church and state of any kind, and may or should endorse some religions (or one specific religion) over others, granting those religions (or that religion) special rights and privileges. For more on preferentialism, see chapter 4. Preferentialism is one of three major positions on church–state issues; it is the opposite of *separationism*, with *accommodationism* representing a compromise between the two views.

Radical feminism The position that simple policy reforms will not be enough to eliminate or satisfactorily address patriarchy, and that *institutional sexism* will continue to exist to an oppressive extent because gender roles, as they presently exist, are inherently oppressive. For more on radical feminism, see chapter 7. Other forms of feminism include *cultural feminism* and *liberal feminism*.

Real liberty The ability of a person to do what he or she wishes to do without impediment, regardless of the source of that impediment. For more on real liberty, see chapter 1.

Rule of law The principle that all persons are subject to the law, and that the power of political leaders to make decisions may be limited by codified law. While the rule of law is never practiced in a pure form, as codified law is always subject to interpretation, basic respect for the rule of law is a fundamental principle of modern government. Government with no concept of the rule of law is called *despotism*. For more on the rule of law, see chapter 2.

Sedition Speech that inspires criticism of, distrust of, or hostility towards the government. For more on sedition, see chapter 3.

Separationism On church–state issues, the position that the government must observe a strict wall of separation of church and state, and must not endorse or support any religion. For more on separationism, see chapter 4. Separationism is one of three major positions on church–state issues, and the strictest of the three; both *accommodationism* and *preferentialism* allow government endorsement of religion to varying degrees.

Sharia Islamic religious law. In a civil liberties context, this is usually used to refer to systems of law based on fundamentalist *Islamist theocracy*. For more on Sharia, see chapter 4.

Sodomy Strictly speaking, sexual penetration of the anus. In a civil liberties context, anti-sodomy laws often ban any form of sexual intercourse viewed as suspect by the government in power, regardless of whether anal penetration is involved. For more on sodomy laws, see chapter 5.

Stolen Generations Australian and Torres Strait children of indigenous ancestry abducted from their families between 1869 and 1976 by the government, or government-endorsed nonprofit organizations, to become wards of the state. For more on the Stolen Generations, see chapter 6.

Theocracy A strongly *preferentialist* government ruled by religious authorities that claims to represent the will of God. For more on theocracies, see chapter 4.

Total Information Awareness (TIA) A data mining program briefly funded by the US Department of Defense in 2002 and 2003 to create and establish a massive database of unknown scope in an effort to root out possible terrorists. The program has frequently been described as *Orwellian*. For more on Total Information Awareness, see chapter 5.

Transgender Transgender persons are those who, through some means or another, identify as persons outside of their assigned gender(s) – usually by adopting the non-assigned gender identity, but sometimes by identifying as androgynous, non-gendered, or multi-gendered. The civil liberties of transgender persons have historically been poorly protected, but this is beginning to change in some liberal democracies. For more on transgender rights, see chapter 7.

Undocumented immigrant Someone who has moved to a country and resides there without having gone through the formal immigration process. Disagreements over the legal status and civil liberties of undocumented immigrants are almost ubiquitous in industrialized nations. For more on undocumented immigrants' rights, see chapter 6.

Utopia An ideal world or nation envisioned and described as the predictably positive long-term result of a given policy or series of policies supported by the deviser. The opposite of a *dystopia*. For more on utopias, see chapter 1.

Zone of privacy The area of one's personal life over which the government has very little legitimate authority. The concept of a zone of privacy is implicit in the Fourth Amendment to the US Constitution, which protects 'the right of a person to be secure in their persons, houses, papers, and effects' against unwarranted searches, but was first explicated in the US Supreme Court's ruling in *Griswold v. Connecticut* (1965), which struck down a state ban on birth control pills.

Index